OUR ORDINARY
EXTRAORDINARY
LIVES

A collection of
Lorian blogs
2015 – 2020

OUR ORDINARY *EXTRAORDINARY* LIVES

A collection of Lorian blogs by

Susan Beal
Claire Blatchford
Drena Griffe
Rue Hass
Mary Reddy
Freya Secrest
Julia Spangler

2015 – 2020

Lorian Press LLC

OUR ORDINARY
EXTRAORDINARY
LIVES

Cover Art by Mary Reddy

Edited by Mary Reddy

Lorian Press LLC
lorianpress.com
lorian.org

ISBN: 978-1-939790-51-4

First Print Edition: August 2021

This book is dedicated to those subtle colleagues and spiritual allies who, working together and in partnership with us, have supported and informed the work of Incarnational Spirituality and Lorian for many years.

Contents

Introduction

How do we live in ways that support not only our own growth but also that of our communities and of the planet? What does it mean to embrace an embodied life that recognizes and honors the life at all levels around us, whether seen or unseen? How do we integrate our experience of inner subtle worlds with the outer physical world? What kind of partnership and collaboration does our world require in order to avoid continual traumatization or the worst effects of unaddressed climate change?

Our blog writers wrestle—and sometimes play—with these questions. They explore topics as diverse as trees and dreams, belly dancing, music and shadows, geomancy, and seeing in the dark. Some challenges are met or chewed over; some moments transformed by beauty—in other words, a chronicle of life as it happens. And the wholeness of that life is enhanced by the attention and intention of each writer as she mulls over the inner and outer workings of her days.

The blogs are loosely arranged by themes but may be dipped into at any point. They were originally posted on the Lorian Association website from 2015 to 2020. Drena Griffe, managing editor of the Lorian blog at this time, was a driving force encouraging us to produce a steady flow of content. She encouraged us to report on how we knit our spiritual practice into our individual lives. She notes that "the point of an incarnational spiritual practice is to willingly partake in the risks of being human."

It's not easy to write about knowledge drawn from a deeply personal intersection of the seen and the unseen, of the somatic, mental, psychic, or intuitive threads of life. I applaud the courage (and sheer doggedness!) that brought each of these accounts into being. And I appreciate the individual lens each writer brings to bear on a topic.

Risk is one lens through which to view our incarnational practice. Another might be relationship—our loving connectedness to every other thing, every being that shares this planet with us. I chose a prism for the cover of this anthology as it aptly expresses the range of personal reflections to be found in these essays. We each refract the light through our unique personalities, shining varied colors into the world. Altogether, the colors become the one light.

As we each process risks, connect in love, and ponder meaning in our own way, we can benefit from hearing how others have proceeded. May our ordinary accounts of the extraordinary richness of life offer you food for thought, inspiration, and perhaps some comfort.

—Mary C. Reddy, editor

What does it mean to lead a sacred life? Perhaps this idea conjures up images of holy men and women, surrounded with clouds of incense, sitting deep in meditation, leading a life dedicated to God, with special clothing and rituals to symbolize and emphasize this dedication. A "sacred life" suggests an otherworldly life divorced from the challenges and temptations of the mundane world.

Incarnational Spirituality is a practice in which living a sacred life means honoring ourselves and the Earth. It is a practice of bringing wholeness into ourselves and into the life of the world around us. It is about engaging through our own uniqueness and blessing with the world as it is, in order that the world as it could be—a loving and healed world—may emerge.

The writers of this book are all engaged in this practice. They write about the many ways in which they bring sacredness into their lives in the midst of the challenges and joys of their everyday world. They write in these blogs about the practice of the "divinely ordinary." In so doing, they illumine what is possible for all of us. They illumine what it can mean to lead a sacred life.

—David Spangler

Chapter 1: Into the Days

Faux Pas in the Deli
Julia Spangler
November 2016

Having been blessed with some acute senses, I move through a world brimming with sights, sounds, and smells. Given that I share that world with a partner who has no sense of smell and is partly deaf, I am especially aware of how much I depend on these senses. Last week my dependence on my nose was brought uncomfortably to my attention.

While in the local grocery store shopping for a crusty bread to complement our dinner, I stood surveying the options. To my pallet, some artisan breads are tastier than others and I depend on my sense of smell to tell me which one to choose. Standing by the array of breads in their bags, I carefully sniffed them, discarding the sour ones and trying to decide between two finalists when a woman nearby said, "People might not appreciate your nose in those bags!"

My response was defensive. "I am drawing air in, not blowing out." In my mind I was being careful, not touching the bread, not contaminating it. We went different directions while I stewed for a bit. Then I asked myself why I was upset. OK. I was embarrassed. Even if I thought I was being careful, I had to admit she had a point. Some people, if not all, might not appreciate my nose so close to bread they would like to buy. Though I was still embarrassed, as I accepted her point of view, I felt the tension I was carrying in my body ease.

My practice when encountering stresses in the world involves first noticing the place in my body where I am feeling uncomfortable, naming the cause, and then allowing my awareness to step back into the space where I can stand in what I sometimes call "Big Julie". This is a felt sense within myself of a wholeness which is more than the specific emotional experience in the moment—in this case, of "embarrassed Julie." I gather into my expansive self the small, embarrassed self with loving forgiveness. This love fills all of those embarrassed spaces, holding them and accepting them. *Yeah, I am not perfect, and that is ok.* I let this love surround and permeate the discomfort in my body, permeate the space around me, and flow out to my sense of the woman who spoke to me. It is from this place where I can love the stranger who caused me distress.

When I got to the checkout lines, there were three to choose from, one of which would take me right behind this woman. Noticing her felt uncomfortable. *Do I hide from her and let this discomfort continue?* It seemed as if she was studiously avoiding seeing me. I decided that I would push through my embarrassment and reach out to my neighbor, perhaps alleviating her probable discomfort at the same time. I pulled into line behind her and touching her gently on the shoulder, getting her attention, I said, "You are right. People might not appreciate my nose in the bags. Thank you for pointing it out to me."

It was not a particularly comfortable moment for either of us. She apologized, I apologized. We found ourselves in that social ritual where each wanted to make the other more comfortable, which was actually difficult under the circumstances. But we could laugh a little. Much better than leaving a small cloud over our shopping experience to linger throughout the day. We did not become friends—there wasn't enough time for that—but I suspect we could have.

To me, this is a form of subtle activism. It is these little daily moments of turning a potential conflict into a moment of connection that can make such a difference in our world.

Skin
Claire Blatchford
January 2016

The waiting room is full today. I check in with the secretary then slip into the last empty chair between a snoozing white-haired man and a young black woman texting hard and fast on her cell phone.

The magazines arranged in even rows on the table reflect the range of ages the dermatologist treats: *AARP, Cosmopolitan, Field and Stream, Good Housekeeping, Reader's Digest, Seventeen, Sports Illustrated.* I find myself wondering if, looking at a section of skin—anybody's skin—just skin and no more, Dr. Gordon could read a brief description, a sort of haiku of that person. In the same way the magazines can be a quick read into one stage or another of life.

Wrinkled, freckled, bumpy in spots but still elastic, certainly well-worn, and, yes, sweetly familiar: I'm suddenly profoundly aware of skin. *My* skin! Eyes, ears and nose I can more or less close or block off. But skin—even when covered over, my skin is on open—always open, exposed, alert.

"Overly dry hands, chapped lips, warm chest, itchy spot on the right rear end, cold blast of air from over there, prickly sore on the forehead," says skin as I reach in my purse for a tube of lotion.

"That ugly sore," I think in reply. "Will Dr. Gordon dig it out? I'm going to a wedding in two days, I don't need a bullet-sized hole in the middle of my face."

"Vain lady!" whispers skin. "Beauty *is* more than skin deep. Beauty is about the health of the whole ..."

As I rub lotion on my hands, skin relaxes and becomes softer. I think of the vast memory of touch skin has gathered within me, not only in my hands and feet, kneeling knees, balancing thighs, tender breasts, but in its constant, simple transparency, no matter how tired or worn. I recall pink flush of babies waking from naps as they return from who knows where, dark circles of sleeplessness, yellow of jaundice, white of fear, blue-black rising up my father's feet from toes to ankles as he began the journey out of his skin.

I recall, not without some embarrassment, how honest skin is. As when I catch sight of someone, someone who "gets under my skin", and instantly feel squirmy irritation. Or how the heat of anger or annoyance can flood into my cheeks. Heck, will I ever be able to get a handle on that? Will I ever be able to brake a blush?

I recall too, how, when I hear something surprising, shocking, even scary, goose bumps often pop up on my arms before I've even processed what I've heard. Goose bumps urging, "Hey! Hey! Wake up! Pay attention!" Even when I'm hearing within by way of intuition rather than through my physical ears. Like remembering someone and seconds later that very someone sends an email.

The arm of the elderly man seated on my left bumps against me. Without looking at him I pull away a bit to give him more space as my awareness shifts from skin as open receiver of an endless stream of information from the outer world, to skin as closed, enclosing, definition of me. I am in here in my body. He is in his body. Skin as limit, border, boundary, anchoring me in this physical incarnation. Thank goodness! Aren't boundaries, in a way, what physical incarnation is all about?

I sink back into my thoughts, my own private room within the waiting room, and wonder: did God doodle me into being using one fluid, loopy, non-stop line? A line that could lengthen, grow, expand, contract, change shape. I hope he had fun! I hope the line—my line—was green, or blue, even changed color as it moved along …

I'm jiggled out of my personal musings as the nurse calls out a name and the man beside me jerks awake, bumping me yet again with his arm, this time a bit harder. I notice then the dark blotches, raised veins, and an ugly red gnash of about three inches on his arm as he staggers to his feet. What a beating his skin has taken—is taking! I'm shocked. I wonder how I missed seeing it.

The young woman to my right stops texting as the white-haired man shuffles past. I feel her wondering, as I am, what happened to him. We exchange a look. As I look at her, I see the pleasing dark smoothness of her skin. Broken, wounded skin on one side, clear, complete skin close by, on the other. I know the difference in the ages of these two has much to do with this outer observation, yet I also know that I do not know—and likely will never know—the boundaries this young woman may experience on many levels because of the color of her skin.

These thoughts flow past as I sense how the mutual sympathy and concern the young black woman and I share for the elderly man have joined and are accompanying him down the hallway to the doctor. It's as though, together, we've drawn, a soft pink bubble around him. And when he's gone out of sight, we share a quick smile. Then return to the privacy and comfort of our own thoughts, our own individual skins.

This brief—really fleeting—experience occurred as I was reading an issue of David Spangler's *Views From the Borderland*. There he speaks of the many "fields within fields" we live and move in every day, all the time, without being aware of them. As I was bothered right then by the prickly sore on my forehead (which turned out to be no big deal) I decided to try tuning in to "skin." And became rather acutely aware not only of my own skin and the skin of others, but the thought that we possess and are constantly moving within and interacting with other, non-physical "skins" or "fields" of thought, feeling and energy.

This is, for me right now, what Incarnational Spirituality is about: as we explore not only the nature of our own personal incarnation but the nature of the earth, the many different worlds and the times we have incarnated into, it's possible to begin to sense, with many senses, the spiritual dimensions within them all.

To close with a quote from David,

"… what happens in my field also happens in the environmental field, the field of humanity, and the planetary field as a whole. It's not that some influence from one field travels across some distance or space to impact another field someplace else; it's that the state of one directly and immediately influences to some extent the state of the other because in mysterious ways, they participate in each other." (Spangler, *Views From the Borderland*, Year 5, Volume III, pp. 6-7)

Thankful for the Teachings of Trains and Toddlers
Rue Hass
March 2019

I have been living with Everett, my two-year-old grandson, all week. I had sort of forgotten how a person just has to surrender 24/7 to experiencing the world the way toddlers do, directly, right now, all the time.

Yesterday we went on a very cool adventure to the Colorado Railroad Museum. Everett is an over-the-top, passionate appreciator of all large machines, and he was in heaven.

He loved the big old trains, and he was entranced with the (comparatively) smaller side cars that used to go along the tracks doing repair work. He could have sat in those all day, engaged with working the levers. He also really liked picking up and investigating the rocks on the ground.

I tried to imagine being Everett, learning to discover, be, and interact with the magic and intelligence of matter. I could feel the intense focus of his awareness: holding an intention to be a body, being present right here, touching, immersing, getting dirty, wondering, understanding. I could feel my own focus on his powerful intention, and also, I could open out to put it into a context, the big picture. Focusing, expanding, focusing, expanding ... feeling the differences, making meaning.

I thought about how this train museum represents so much of humanity's history of exploring the material realm. How much we have learned, how profoundly we have shaped the world, for better and worse; how broad the possibilities, how narrow our perspective. Also, how vibrant our imagination is. From waking to sleeping, every day we practice framing our relationship with the ancient intelligence of matter.

I remembered something that David Spangler had said (during the 2013 Integrative Forum: The Chalice of Self):

"The soul takes incarnation for several reasons. One of them is to come into contact with and engage with the phenomenon of physical matter. We may think of matter simply as a dense thing or condition, something with which we have to contend during our incarnation. But in fact, matter is an intelligence and an ancient and powerful one at that. We see the outlines and 'thinking' of this intelligence in the laws and principles of physics and chemistry (which in turn give rise to the principles of biology), but matter is more than just these laws and principles. It is an intent, one that allows a whole realm to come into existence, and it is the presence from which this intent emerges or perhaps more precisely, it is the presence and intelligence that allows this intent to express."

As we go through our lives, we may not think much of matter itself except when it gets in our way or we feel its burden. We all have an intuition that our souls don't have to deal with the characteristics of physical matter and consequently enjoy what to us seems like a state of greater freedom and grace. But from the soul's perspective, the intelligence of matter is like an ancient elder, a wise one or master. Just as my personality might travel to the Himalayas or to some other mythic place (India? Glastonbury?) to find and sit in the presence of an adept, so the soul travels to sit in the presence of an adept, so the soul travels into the incarnate realm to be with the presence of Matter and to learn what it has to teach it.

Machines are a pretty new creation in human history. They are the birth child of matter and its willing interaction with the expansive yet limited vision of humans. These big old trains were super cool in their time. Look how we get around now!

I turned my attention back to Everett, inspecting a piece of coal that has fallen from an old train's furnace. He is just as fascinated by the chunk of coal as he is by what he can produce with his adept touch on the screen of his mom's tablet device, switching between his favorite cartoon programs. She and I often marvel that at two he already has this sophisticated computer technology handled.

Humanity's evocative partnership with machines will create more and more powerful technology. Its future is unimaginable to us. We need as much conscious awareness, appreciation, flexibility, and love as we can muster. Our future depends on it. I reach for Everett's beautiful dirty hand, loving him so much, and I give thanks for his opportunity to be in the presence of Matter, learning what it has to teach him, and me.

Our future is in good hands.

Your Calling Is to Be Here
Julia Spangler
February 2017

"Your calling is to be here. There is no higher mission, for each of us is a gateway that can open to allow the Beloved to step through. To give expression to the Beloved, to be that gateway, is why the universe appeared. It is the ultimate Call." —David Spangler

One day when my daughter Kaiti was about five years old we were driving home together, just the two of us. As often happens at such times when we are alone with our children, our conversation was more intimate than usual. Sometimes personally, sometimes philosophically, sometimes answering questions. The question that came up that day was "Who is your favorite child?"

Anyone who has more than one child does their best to not play favorites. For me, with our four kids, there was not one that was better than another. Sure, they were all different from each other, and each provided his or her own challenges designed to push parental buttons. But each one is equally treasured for who they are, unique and individual. And each child reflected his and her own individuality even before birth, each one coming in with their own personality and their own different individual needs.

I was always aware that this particular child came in with a need to feel special. Kaiti once told me that she, the third among four, should have been an only child. I thought this recognition of her need for complete attention was a remarkably astute bit of self awareness for one so young. (And I reminded her that in that case she should have chosen a different family, as her brothers were here first—which gave her pause.)

So this day, on this drive, when this child asked me, "Who do you love the most?" … many responses ran through my mind: the diplomatic "I have no favorite, of course!"; the tease, "Aidan!" (wink wink); the affirming, "You are my favorite"; or even the tuneful, "The one I am with." What I did instead was ask her a question back. "Are you wanting me to say you, sweetie?"

Her answer surprised me a bit at first, but then it didn't. "No!" she said, tearing up, "Because I would feel bad for the others if you loved me more!" We went on to discuss the different ways we love and the ways we can love different people. The love may not be exactly the same, but it is quantitatively just as much.

We all need to feel that we matter. Some traditions liken this need to egotism, an over-inflated sense of self which we must guard against: "I need to be more important than everyone else." It may be there in some part of the ID or even part of the survival coding in our DNA. But I think the need to matter is also embedded in the inborn function which creates identity — that part of us which can say not only "I AM" but also "I AM HERE". It gives rise to the need to be seen, to be loved, and is a response to the deep innate need to be part of something that is bigger than us.

In his book *The Call* (Lorian Press, *2015)*, David Spangler says that we matter because we are here and especially when we can be fully consciously here. The call to be part of something bigger than ourselves is actually the call that we answered when we took life. And that call is, to quote David, "the call to treasure and value and love one another and all the other creatures and things of the earth. It is the call to acknowledge and to act from that knowledge that each person is just as valued and just as loved as the next, and all are invited to participate in the communion of that love."

A deep call from spirit may not be a call to do something specific and spectacular. It may simply be a call to show up and love. In our home, whichever of our children shows up when the front door opens and they come in, a warm and loving shout of greeting meets them. When we show up, love is there to greet us, and we matter.

"The call actually comes from the person standing in front of you, who in their heart of hearts is saying "Will you … value me? … Will you see the sacred in me, the sovereignty in me? It is my action in response to that call that draws me into a loving space. It is what opens me to experience the background call of the universe." —David Spangler

Lessons in Mirror Are Closer Than They Appear
Drena Griffith
September 2018

Last week I nearly lost my car—and in the midst of discomfort recovered some valuable lessons in being human.

On Tuesday evening, thieves broke into my 2006 Subaru. I awoke to a broken hood, disabled alarm, and the car's ignition switch dangling from the steering column. All things considered, I'm lucky I woke up to any car at all! Ironically, at the beginning of this month I moved from an apartment complex in a deteriorating part of my community to a private garden level on the other side of town.

On the surface the situation unfolds as one might expect: expensive repairs and unexpected delays, not to mention the need to purchase an immobilizer to ward off future theft attempts (apparently older model Subarus are blue light specials to thieves because they deliver high value in the stolen car market and are relatively easy to steal).

No one appreciates a violation of their personal space, and I'm certainly no exception—but at the same time, as a person who looks upon the world with spiritual eyes, I cannot help asking the question, "What might I learn from this situation?"

I tend to approach all difficulties, especially unexpected life occurrences, as opportunities for reflection. Having said that, this situation in particular has not been easy. For one thing, it's been a long year. Seems like one life-learning opportunity after another has steadily piled itself outside my door.

Though it pains me to admit it, on some level I've been waiting for all of these unexpected deliveries from the universe to magically dematerialize so that I could shake off the dust, all lessons learned. If pressed, of course I would never suggest that there ever comes any point in time when people, no matter how spiritual, become immune to occurrences of life. Did I buy into the idea that the spiritual path might itself be a protection against upset, inconvenience, pain—even temporarily?

When I confessed these feelings to a friend, she said, wisely, "Drena, I think you need to … expand your perceptions." So I did.

For the past several days I've been sitting with the situation, reflecting upon it and allowing it to communicate with me as I would a loved one. The opportunity to expand our perceptions is perhaps the real gift of any difficulty we face. In my case, widening the view has revealed some unexpected insights

First off, the practical, grounded view: everything is a tradeoff

In connecting with my new neighbors, I've learned there's a higher rate of car theft in this safe, upper-middle class environment. Vehicles are regularly trashed and tousled for valuables. "No matter how safe, this is still urban America," a new acquaintance offered wryly.

Conversely, the working-class complex I left had a higher rate of social violence. In fact, safety became the decisive issue inspiring my relocation. So now it seems I've traded one concern for another. With full awareness I can assess and accept this new risk because it was my choice to move, just as it is my choice to live in such a large city to begin with. Grounding my perspective in the particular details of my environment allows me to stand in a space of empowerment, rather than victimization.

Which leads to my second, more spiritual view: choice is the apex of Incarnational Spirituality.

If we strip Lorian principles down to their wires, then we must acknowledge that, at the core, every being reveals the power of incarnation. Every person inherently possesses a spark of the impulse (that some call God, Source, the Sacred, the Divine, Big Bang, etc.) which infuses creation.

But if this is true, then how do we account for the seemingly endless list of examples of human beings misusing their spark? What separates the villains from the saints?

Actually, Julia Spangler and I debate these finer points on occasion, and this is the place where we inevitably get stuck. If everyone and everything reveals the sacred impulse of God, then at what point does Incarnational Spirituality become a practice rather than an idea?

Simply stated, at the point of choice.

Choice is the crux of sovereignty. We each get access to an assortment of decisions and possibilities. My spiritual practice is revealed by how I carry myself through the world, not by how the world interacts with me.

Especially in the metaphysical community, I think there's an assumption that the more spiritual we are, the smoother our lives tend to flow. Or stated another way, the better we are at our spirituality, the less impact the material world will have on us. We tend to approach the difficulties of life as symptoms of spiritual "dis-ease." If we're sick, it's because we have unresolved childhood issues calcifying in our bodies. If we're poor, it's due to unreleased beliefs around scarcity. If bad things happen to us, then we're clearly doing something wrong, and there are any number of meditations, reflections, tinctures, readings, and healers to help us get back on the right track! Certainly, any and all situations can be opportunities to heal, to improve and to reassess—but as the old saying goes, "The rain falls on the just and the unjust."

So what if difficulties are occasions to practice making choices which ultimately can inspire us and those around us to live meaningful, more purposeful lives?

Which culminates into my final, aerial view: how we choose to interpret and live in the world mirrors back to the world

Regularly, I do check-ins with colleagues on the healing path; this past weekend we connected and I opened up about the car theft and other recent stresses. It was pointed out that I have difficulty receiving. "You are someone capable of giving, but you don't allow yourself to receive from others. You need to learn how to ask for help and to let others care for you."

Confession: for a moment I thought, somewhat sardonically, *So ... the universe let my car get broken into and nearly stolen and now I'm saddled with a thousand dollars in repairs so that I can learn how to ... receive?*

But I shook these thoughts off because, well, the universe didn't cause anything to happen to my car. Life happened to my car. (Or, rather, thieves happened upon my car conveniently located on the corner.) In considering the point my colleagues made, though, I had to admit that it's true I don't like asking for assistance. Needing help does make me uncomfortable. Initially, waking up last week to a stripped car felt like the final straw. More so than a violation of space, it seemed like an attack upon my independence and ability to take responsibility for my own needs so that I could ... avoid reaching out for others?

So, relaxing into this discomfort, I gazed into the proverbial mirror held up before me and noticed a number of peripheral blessings:

—Upon learning about the break-in and attempted theft, my

boyfriend immediately rearranged his schedule to be of assistance.

—I had to cancel several appointments at the last minute and my clients and friends were kind and understanding.

—I received a referral for a towing company that offered a generous rate; also, in spite of the damage and state of the car, the tow itself went smoothly, without any glitches.

—My regular mechanic kept the car for several days and ultimately wasn't able to get the parts to complete the repair; yet he helped me get the car to a specialty Subaru shop and did not charge me any fee.

—The Subaru shop loaned me an Outback to drive while they repair the damage.

Last week I chose to park my car on the street outside my new apartment. Last week car thieves (thankfully, unsuccessfully) chose to steal it. Ever since then friends and clients and mechanics and tow truck drivers and colleagues have made choices that continue supporting me. And I get to choose to receive these blessings and hidden gifts. I also get to choose to interact with this experience in a way that affirms the world, not as I wish it to be, but as I want to be

From this vantage point, it seems impossible to not recognize the truth that how we see the events of our lives impacts the quality and care we bring to every moment. Ultimately, I think the point of an incarnational spiritual practice is to willingly partake in the risks of being human and in the process to recognize that we can change the world by giving it the opportunity to impact us.

Ordinary Ecstasy
Mary Reddy
January 2016

One Christmas Eve when I was sixteen, I went with my mother and my youngest brother to our local parish church for Midnight Mass. After driving through quiet suburban streets, we pulled into a parking lot that could have belonged to a shopping mall. I stepped out of the car and looked toward the church. Such a plain building—dun-colored bricks and a slightly arched roof with only a tall thin cross at the entrance to announce that it was a church.

The story was that the parishioners had modeled the squat building after a gymnasium, thinking to use it for worship until they saved the funds to build a real church. Then, voila, they'd have a gym for the adjacent grade school. Of course, years passed with no new church. Instead, this ordinary building continued to serve the ethereal.

Over half of the members of our family must have decided to stay home that evening. Instead of seven people piling out of the car, it was just the three of us. The air was appropriately crisp; an indigo heaven of stars vaulted above us. Yet I don't remember feeling anything much but the ordinariness of walking across the parking lot to attend the service.

But then I happened to glance at my mother and brother as we neared the church, and I was suddenly startled by a rush of love. For a timeless moment, a light shone about the three of us and sweet music accompanied our steps. In that moment, these two dear people held all I knew of love on earth and in the heavens. And I felt something akin to the love one finds in the trenches, that deep connection among those who have held together through difficult times—as if our lives were a quest and we were each other's noble companions. I was held in a moment of ecstasy, knowing that they existed and that we could be together, however long or short a time we might be given.

Some years later I found myself in an off-campus apartment with a few college friends. I had wandered away from the conversation and walked toward the window, feeling a great weariness that hung on my limbs and nestled in my heart. I stared out at a muffled sky the color of lint. From this third-floor window I looked across to the bare limbs of an old elm tree. Nothing stirred; it was a still grey day. Nothing I saw cut through my fatigue and my lack of hope.

But then I caught some movement down below, a bit of color. Across the street at ground level, I saw a little girl, a toddler dressed in bright pink, pressing her face against a window of her house. I wondered if she wanted to play outside and was waiting for permission. Suddenly, the world shifted. I felt myself flying down to meet her, the two of us running together into the world to play. With untrammeled joy, sweet curiosity and breathless expectation—we were completely at home in the river of moments which are life. I was flooded with love. I loved that little girl and I loved the little girl I had once been. My love rippled out in waves, encompassing my friends who still sat in animated conversation across the room. My love stretched beyond to the little girl's house, to the elm tree, the neighborhood, and the flat grey sky. I was transformed.

These moments that live in my memory transported me into the Sacred. They lifted a veil to reveal how extraordinary the ordinary really is. Sometimes nature can evoke the same bright joy in me. It might be waves rushing onto the wet sand, then sucking back to sea or a cloudscape of grey, white, and smoky blue shot with gold. At the core of these experiences is my loving awareness of the moment.

But what about the many non-ecstatic moments that make up the bulk of my life? As I tap at my laptop, cook meals, read books, talk, sleep, cry, sigh, laugh, cough, blow my nose, wash my clothes—without ecstasy but with a quiet surety—I look for that deep sense of the sacredness of all life and of my own sacred presence within it as an essential participant. When no mystic vision arrives to transport me, I have found I can begin by connecting with myself. That self-acknowledgement—here I am!— wakes up my appreciative attention to all the beings with which I share this moment, whether human, plant, mineral, animal, or delightfully "other." Here I am, with all of you!

I'm reminded of a passage in J. D. Salinger's short story "Teddy" that describes just such a realization of the extraordinary love present in our ordinary moments. Teddy sees his little sister drinking her milk and suddenly he saw that "she was God and the milk was God. I mean, all she was doing was pouring God into God." Think of it. In our profound connectedness within the web of life, it's true for all of us. All we are doing is pouring God into God.

Baring Belly and Soul:
Belly Dancing and Incarnational Spirituality
Rue Hass
January 2016

Five years ago, I signed up for what I thought would be a fun way to get some exercise for a few weeks by learning about belly dance. I could not have predicted (and would have fled from!) the idea that it would turn out that I was joining a belly dance performing troupe ... that would have me up on stage in front of hundreds of people ... baring my belly! OMG!

Belly dance in its essence is a celebration of the radiance and power of the body. It is powerful core work that requires and develops strength and flexibility. I have always loved dancing, and I have a good sense of rhythm and flow. But I found it brought up interesting challenges for me. First came my (and everywoman's, every person's) personal drama about body image stuff. And then there is being willing to be so visible while doing something I will never be really good at.

Belly dancing does not come easily for me. I am sort of challenged by my particular body shape, and scoliosis in my spine, along with the effects of 72 years of life (that's another thing—I am the oldest person in my class, and probably in the whole troupe of some 75 women of all ages and sizes). I watch the strong, lithe, flexible bodies of the teacher and the younger women in my group with love, longing, and deep, deep appreciation.

I learn best by watching the teacher's body make the moves, and then I practice finding the essence of those moves in my own experience, getting my body to take a shape that feels like what I see in her. That is how I learned Tai Chi many years ago. It is a good learning strategy. But—I have the funny experience of feeling each particular belly dance phrase moving perfectly through me, and then I look in the mirror and see that what I feel on the inside doesn't make me look like her! I am not just "comparing and falling short" here. It is an interesting meditation on learning, exploring, accepting, and creating with my own subtle energy body language.

And learning complicated choreography is hard for me. My mind works fluidly, intuitively. Choreography is a linear organization of specific moves. The teacher's strategy is to help students to become proficient in the individual belly dance moves, and from there, learn how to improvise. At the beginning I think I am never going to be able to learn the dance. It really requires that I open to hearing, feeling, and seeing the music in some inner way. I need to let my body find it, and let it find my body. My mind and earnest intentions and even practice can't do this alone.

A good example is our performances last autumn of a Zombie belly dance to the Michael Jackson song "Thriller" based on Jackson's original dance moves. What a thought—to be the living dead, with rhythm!

"Thriller" was the hardest belly dance I have learned, with many advanced moves. It required being dead and alive, precise and loose, at the same time. I had to kind of let myself bypass any philosophical disagreements I might have with the song (to say nothing of the blood and ghoulishness) so I could participate in the lively fun and outrageousness. The audiences loved it! Who knew it was such fun to be dead?

(The living dead, belly dancing, the postmortem realms—it all collides in my head!)

In the weeks before last year's performance show in May, called "She-Nanigans," (with stage lighting, announcers, filming, yikes!), the teacher asked each of us in the troupe to write something about our experience of belly dance to be read out at various times during the show.

I thought about the history of belly dance as a deep honoring of the wisdom of the earth and the body, through women especially. I thought of how the Sidhe bring life into being through song and dance. I asked that they, and all my inner allies and Gaia, help me to move my focus beyond being so anxious about making a fool of myself on stage, to allowing the music to move the dance through me.

I thought about how learning the dances and preparing for our big annual show and other performances has been an opportunity for me to practice moving in this embodied incarnation with creative acceptance and flow.

Here is what I wrote:

"In order to be freely ourselves, and truly touch a happy creative flow of life, we need to ground ourselves in the land under our feet and the stars above us. That grounding forms a nourishing support for weaving the complex rhythms of life and the patterns of emotion that we embody. Joy, lightness, and heart-full courage arise from here. Now we can offer form to the irrepressible shenanigans of spirit."

Belly dancing through the lens of Incarnational Spirituality has helped me to stand strong in myself, to hold a space for my unique individuality, and to co-create with intention and love. It is helping me to dance my spirit into being.

Sing the Song in Your Heart
Mary Reddy
February 2019

In fifth grade, the nuns taught us to read music. They counted music as an essential member of the family whose siblings were reading, writing, and mathematics. After a year of studying the treble clef; whole, half, and quarter notes; rhythms and key signatures, we each had to pass a final sight-reading exam. When it was my turn, I stood up and sang to my classmates from a piece of sheet music that I'd never seen before. I had the curious sensation of being terrified that people were looking at me mingled with the surety that I could do this! It was not my anxious mind that succeeded, it was my voice and my eyes in sync, acting together to vocalize the visual and spatial relationships I saw on the page before me. I passed the exam.

In grade school, I sang alto in the church choir. It often meant learning counterintuitive melodies that underlined or counterpointed the primary melody. I loved these sounds that felt all the more powerful because they sat back behind the song, underpinning it, providing a shadow to its light so that the whole was more clearly etched in the listener's heart.

But for much of my life, music was the lover that got away. I enjoyed brief periods with the piano as a child and later in young adulthood with the guitar followed by years of simply listening to others play. But when alone listening to recorded music, I have always sung along. If I love a song, I cannot stay silent; I raise my voice to sound the notes. And now I am seeking out that love once more, not to abandon it again.

For that love is a sacred communion. Over the centuries, people instinctively sensed the spiritual power of song—as hymns, psalms, and chants woven into rituals, augmented by drums or musical instruments. One of my aunts wrote liturgical music on the piano but was adamant that the human voice itself was the best instrument to praise God. I regret that I never asked her why she thought that. But in musing about the sacredness of sound, it occurred to me that the human voice is a unique incarnational instrument.

First, consider the impact of music on the body. In recent studies, neuroscientists have discovered that multiple parts of the brain light up when listening to music. The musicians themselves show even more intense brain activity especially in the areas governing auditory, visual, and motor functions. Though fewer studies have been done on the effects of singing on the brain, they reveal a similar increased activity across multiple areas of the brain.

Outside the brain, singing engages over a hundred muscles around the vocal cords, the larynx, the trachea, and the lungs, creating vibrations fueled by breath, changing pitch by speeding up or slowing down the vibratory frequency, adjusting volume by working the breath through the resonating passages of the throat, mouth, and nose. The listening ears are also involved to sense the quality of the sound and the accuracy of the pitch as it's produced. And think of how that sound is heard by the singer both externally and internally as it resonates within the singer's skull.

The vagus nerve, the "wanderer," is the longest cranial nerve linking the brain to the rest of the body. It connects to the vocal cords, the muscles in the back of the throat, as well as to the diaphragm which works the bellows of the lungs. It's no surprise that studies suggest singing, humming, and chanting improve the tone of the vagus nerve, helping us to access the "rest and recover" mode when needed. The vagus nerve regulates things below the level of consciousness—another hint as to the sacred power of song, for it engages much more of us than just our conscious mental process.

Thus, singing is healing for us as it calls forth a great deal of energy and interaction within the body. But how are we to define its sacred qualities? Songs have the power to open our hearts to a range of deep emotions—intensifying our human experience. And music of any kind creates sounding boards in the environment. Things resonate in kind. I was fascinated by this twin effect, both on the person singing and on the singer's environment. But I still wondered about the sacredness of song. What happens in the subtle realms when a person sings?

One day while working with the Sidhe cards, I asked to understand how singing evokes the sacred. I found myself creating the stone circle within me, inside my body. I became aware of the Grail that I am, that we each are. I (somewhat impatiently) thought, "Yes, the Grail, but how does this relate to song?" Then I saw the vibratory tones of song resonating within this Grail then flowing out to the world. It seems, in singing, we partake in the circulatory system of the world on both ordinary and subtle levels. I later learned my friend Anne Gambling had synchronistically put into words what I saw in this attunement: singing is "the means to 'dig the trench' for liquid light to flow, further, wider, deeper each time."

Singing knits our spirits and bodies together in a coherent resonance but doesn't stop there, as the song moves out of our bodies into the air, sending out waves in increasing circles to engage with everything in the vicinity. I sensed that singing can be an alchemical act, translating the music of the spheres through flesh and blood, then flowing out to the surrounding environment.

We may envision our grail selves as containers, holding the Sacred. But David Spangler emphasizes that this is not a passive function. And he chose a musical analogy to explain that the Grail is an active presence, a sacred doing. "Think of it as analogous to a 'violin self' a consciousness within you that loves to play the violin … as you practice, you will be able to 'hold' and play ever more complex pieces of music. … so we have in the grail a sacramental instrument, one that delivers and shares sacredness in a communion of being." Perhaps the sacredness of song resides in this process of both holding and sharing.

In David's *Conversations with the Sidhe* (Lorian Press, June 2014), his Sidhe colleague Mariel says we carry within us "the memory of the telluric technology of node, connection, and flow, shaped by song and dance and ritual." Raising our own voices in song activates the flow from node to node, enhancing the harmony and coherence of our world. And the Singing Hare exhorts us, "Wake then, listen, hear again the song of life and the song of being amidst the fields of your daily life. Will you join in the sing? … Stand under the dome of heaven if you dare and let the song well up in you, silent or loud." (*The Sidhe Oracle of the Fleeting Hare*, John Matthews and Will Kinghan, Lorian Press, June 2018)

Learning to Be All In with Life
Freya Secrest
March 2019

My new granddaughter, Kaileia, is three months old and beginning to explore her muscle control and coordination. She lives in the present moment, actively engaging with all that comes her way. I partnered in her world of discovery recently and the ripples of that experience live in me as an extraordinary example of presence and communication.

That afternoon, she had been playing on her own, thoughtfully, slowly moving her arms to connect with a hanging mobile. Sometimes she touched and grabbed it, sometimes not. Her full attention seemed to be concentrated on that toy, but she held no specific idea to do anything with it or to it. Instead, it seemed Kaileia was exploring the space around it, feeling into a broader field of engagement. She was using every physical and somatic sense she could access for her learning.

I picked Kaileia up from the floor and held her in my arms in a position that allowed us to see each other. I was the focus of her attention now and with her eyes, her interest, her body, she directed herself toward our interaction. We started a conversation.

As I talked to her and entered more fully into the field defined by our eye contact and physical touch, my speech slowed, and I focused on key words and sounds rather than long sentences. Her attention sharpened; she was a partner ready to engage. Watching Kaileia respond, I slowed down even further and settled even more into my body and subtle senses. I noticed her mouth movements as she tasted the air of our communication and began to mimic them, trying to taste it too. Shaping my mouth slowly into an O, I put more breath into it and it became a note of sound; she lit up. I began singing more slow notes and she began to mimic my mouth very specifically. Her eyes were glued to my face as she worked to move her own mouth and make the sounds I was making. And she did it! Of course, I and the others around gave delighted praise. It was a doorway moment for her and for me that recognized our connection.

What followed was several minutes of call and response and deep belly laughs from both of us as we lived into the delight of this moment of conscious communication. Kaileia was almost ecstatic to feel her participation in the exchange. The world opened up to her; she made a difference. I was in awe of what was possible within the gift of becoming present. Everyone in the room was transformed with her joy.

What I take away from that exchange, besides my grandmotherly pride in a brilliant grandchild, is an experience of being "all in" and the value of being somatically alert and responsive to my world. This deeper sense of presence resonates and moves through me as simple, direct, honest, with a fullness of joy that links body, mind, emotion and spirit. Kaileia brings all of herself to her work as a young incarnating soul in the world; she has a task to connect and establish and grow a life. I feel that same responsibility and am appreciating the reminder to bring myself humbly and expectantly to the task.

This state of wonder and magic seems particularly appropriate in my work with subtle energies and a living universe. I am inspired to taste the air of my attunements, to let my arms wave and give shape to my experiences. Kaileia is my poster child for "all in". I look up from my computer screen and see my neighbor's tall pine. My back straightens and head lifts. I move into a felt sense of height that perhaps is more akin to the tree's experience. Like my granddaughter, I try to shape myself to imitate its song. In this brief exchange I feel joy coursing through my uprightness. Perhaps this is a moment of tree-speak.

This somatic languaging is a rich addition to my subtle world communication. It has been part of our teaching in Incarnational Spirituality but this experience calls me to further recognize and harness its power. I find a more tangible sense of where to meet and engage with fellow Gaian beings—both those in physical form and those in subtler embodiment. Slowing down enough to focus with interest on what is in front of me, I stand in present moment. Welcoming the light of multiple perspectives, the present flows with greater clarity and connectedness. Delighting in our connection, we are communicating, and the fabric of life is enhanced.

This experience with Kaileia has illustrated a new fullness and aliveness in my life. I have no nouns to describe it firmly yet. But while it is still a mystery to me, the somatic doorway that she modeled is woven more strongly into the fabric of my awareness.

Ashes
Drena Griffith
March 2017

On Ash Wednesday, for the first time in a long while, I attended Mass. For the past several weeks I have felt a strong stirring to revisit the Catholicism of my childhood, yet as a Lorian priest representing Incarnational Spirituality and also a member of a local Native community, I'm not entirely sure how to integrate all of these multifaceted, jigsaw pieces of my spiritual experience. It's all still unfolding for me. Regardless, the first day of Lent felt an especially appropriate time to lean more deeply into this exploration.

Lent is, for me, a time for remembering, for focusing on important things inadvertently forgotten or lost in the details of living a busy, stressful life. It is also an opportunity to "re-member" — to call back the scattered pieces of myself and listen to the quiet voice of the soul. Lent is about centering and returning to "right relationship" with the world. This year it seems I have more scattered pieces than I realized.

As a child I loved being Catholic. Regularly I memorized songs and prayers and reenacted the sacred rites in playtime. I was also rather precocious spiritually and had very high expectations: of myself, of God — of life in general. So I asked many questions of God and the nuns at my church. As I got older those questions became more intense and the pat responses I had accepted at ten stopped making sense. It wasn't that I had any agenda or attachment to particular answers, but I desperately needed my faith to have a certain stability and solidity that, looking back, I can see my earlier years in general lacked. When a classmate at college insisted that she had found that assurance I was seeking and invited me to attend an evangelical service, I was skeptical, but curious enough. See, I never really consciously intended to leave the Catholic church, but when the evangelicals promised me answers, promised me peace, I believed. Then the shackles came out … and on *that* story goes, for a decade. By the time I found the exit door, apart from one or two good friends, I didn't leave with much I'd ultimately decide to keep. I swore I was done with Jesus, Faith, and Answers. Well, that clearly didn't last. At least not the first two, though my relationships with both have definitely evolved.

As has my connection to Mass. Sitting in the sanctuary on Wednesday morning felt both familiar and completely foreign. For one thing, the church of my childhood was a hermitage compared to this labyrinthine structure. Hundreds of people were in attendance, and that service was one of a half dozen offered throughout the day. The rituals were, thankfully, the same, though some of the recitations have changed. I felt awkward. Exposed.

As a holy day of obligation, Ash Wednesday takes its name from the ritual marking of parishioners' foreheads with ashes. This symbol of penance demarcates the season. "Remember that you are dust, and to dust you shall return," said Father Felix, marking my forehead with a sideways cross that covered nearly all of my brow with soot.

After so many years of renunciation, was repentance and reconciliation possible now? Perhaps more importantly, what was I even attempting to reconcile? I realized that the last Ash Wednesday service I had attended prior to my unconscious abandonment had been when I was eighteen, a senior in high school. Was I attempting to reconnect, not just with an old faith, but with an old me? An old me with wide eyes that attended Mass week after week alone—without parents or sibling—prompted by nothing but the stirrings of her open heart? An old self with soul-stirring dreams and seemingly limitless potential? Well, that was definitely a long time ago, before I lost faith in myself and became so consumed with finding the right spiritual answers that in the process, I *willingly* gave away everything I felt in that open heart to be true. Way leads onto way ... as Cherokee Strong Eyes said, "We can't go back. The bridge is gone."

Even so, I obviously attended Mass looking for something. For that matter, what do I go to Native Lodge looking for? And how does Incarnational Spirituality, which celebrates the individual life as inherently sacred, integrate with a faith where any discussion of the individual starts with sin and ends with the need to apologize? How does a Lorian priest wear a forehead covered in ash?

According to my Native teacher, Coyo, this time of the year is known as the Void. We're nearly through the dark of the year, so our minds and spirits are turning toward spring, facing forward with resolve toward fresh growth. Yet winter isn't quite done with us yet. The seeds within are still turning. It's not quite time for us to take action. Instead, we sit with our desires and longings, sit with whatever stirs and strives within us. Then we allow those stirrings and strivings themselves to be cut open, revealing the wounds beneath and the hidden paths waiting to be reclaimed. If we move too quickly to action, we disrupt the process. So we must patiently and gently hold the seeds. We must attend to our inner needs so that what our souls want to grow can most fully align with the conditions of our lives when the time for growing comes. In spite of the stirrings of transition, now is not the time for decisions or answers. We are still incubating our new selves in the dark.

I was reminded of Coyo's words as Father Felix gave the homily: immediately following Christ's baptism, this most sacred spiritual initiation, he was led by God into the desert where he fasted for 40 days and nights. Isolated. Exposed. Incubated. Even Christ had questions and doubts. Even Christ experienced the void.

Bare bones honest: as a teenager and young adult I was never going to find the assurances I was seeking in my childhood faith, but there's no way I could have known that then. The issues weighing on my heart at that time weren't questions of belief so much as questions of life that I was making God responsible for because I didn't know where else to turn. At eighteen I felt powerless and like so many vulnerable lost souls, I placed my trust in someone, in many other someones who, in order to *save* me gladly took from me the power I didn't realize I had.

But even my odyssey into evangelical Christianity was a sign of a deeper misalignment. I was never going to find answers in any religion, really, because that's not what religion is for. We can only find our answers in direct relationship with the Sacred—in deep, abiding connection with ourselves. Faith is the tool we use to express our innate understanding of sacredness. Ironically, I have heard this core message, in one convoluted form or another, in nearly every church and spiritual center I've ever been part of. I am only now beginning to understand.

Ash Wednesday turned out to be a day full of great meaning and insight. And for the forty-six days and nights of Lent, I will be paying attention. Sitting in quietude and stillness, I will, as Rainer Marie Rilke suggests, lean into and learn to love the questions stirring within. In spite of the darkness of the void, I feel open to releasing the jigsaw puzzle of my past to this newly emerging self still sleeping in her seed.

Grateful for the Gin Joint
Mary Reddy
November 2015

What exactly do we do when we give thanks? Many indigenous tales and, recently, even articles in business publications describe the positive ripple effects of practicing gratitude. But what does that practice look like?

Wandering on the Internet, examining definitions, anthropological studies, and self-help columns on gratitude, I was struck by a quote from an unfamiliar source: David Graeber. I discovered he is an American anthropologist, a professor at the London School of Economics, a political activist and author of *Debt: The First 5,000 Years*. (Graeber, Melville House, July 2011)

Graeber wrote: "Exchange encourages a particular way of conceiving human relations." He goes on to say that exchange implies equality, but it also implies separation. That implied separation opened up for me a meditation on thankfulness.

We give thanks for things we have—good health, a roof overhead, food to eat, family and friends. We give thanks for gifts. And yet, if we only offer thanks in return for a gift, do we secretly feel indebted to the giver?

The vocabulary of "giving" and "having" implies a separateness and a need to achieve balance to preserve equality. Suppose we push the concept of gratitude beyond this give-and-take? Instead of exchange across separation, can we simply be with that which we are thankful for? Participating in the value of what we appreciate, we may also find a way to thank ourselves, both for being and for being with this valued person or thing.

A friend of mine, a former therapist who worked with troubled teens, used to council parents to practice what he called the "Be By" method. A parent's best expression of love and support for a teenager, he said, was to be nearby—whether to listen or sit in silence—to simply be by their child, offering the precious gifts of time and attention. It is a kind of holding, an opening which creates a space. What a message of thankfulness that space conveys! A thankfulness which participates in the being of another.

Imagine, instead of saying thanks, sitting (like a parent, like a lover) with that which you are grateful for. Being by—no exchange across a separation—just a quiet joyful attentiveness, in wonder and gratitude.

This practice expands to thankfully inhabiting oneself; to being by, in, and with yourself. No list making is required. A strictly mental approach will not get you there. Gratitude as a state of being will emerge from the love you hold for yourself as a sovereign being and, by extension, the love you radiate to other beings by simply valuing being alive and present to them.

Can you conjure up the feeling of a time when you were utterly glad to be alive? It was probably not a moment inspired by separation, more likely one sparked by connection and love, whether for another person, a beautiful landscape, or a beloved animal. Perhaps you tingled with heightened awareness, sensing that relationship is at the heart of all that inspires gratitude in us.

What if you cannot conjure up such a feeling? Perhaps you are sunk in pain or grief or exhausted by the challenges of your life. Try this: imagine you are the hero of your life's movie and it's not going so well! In the 1942 American film, Casablanca, Rick bemoans the appearance of his lost love, Ilsa, who enters his bar with another man. "Of all the gin joints, in all the towns, in all the world, she walks into mine." He rails against the random fate that reunites them yet as time goes by, in that reunion, they learn each other's secrets, heal their broken hearts, and devote themselves to a higher cause.

When I am confronted with a not-so-lovely-to-me person or a trying situation, I think to myself, "of all the gin joints!" I know that, like it or not, work will be done, veils pulled back, muscles stretched, and new selves will emerge. The gin joint reminds me of the love inherent in every life situation, even the ones which appear to be unwanted or deeply tragic. After all, your enemy is your greatest teacher–a person to be grateful for.

Practicing gratitude is not so different from opening to love—love of yourself, your favorite coffee cup, a maple tree burning red in autumn, voices raised in song, a well-known crack in the sidewalk, an annoying neighbor, an enemy, a best friend. Practicing gratitude as a whole and emergent lover of life, you may discover thankfulness resides in your every breath, in and out.

The Gift of Light
Julia Spangler
December 2018

Once again it is the Season of Light in my world. Christmas, Hanukah, Diwali, Winter Solstice in the northern hemisphere—all are festivals held at this time of year celebrating the return of the Light from the long darkness. In my household we have always celebrated both the Winter Solstice and Christmas, while holding respect for all others

The Winter Solstice has been precious to me ever since I lived in northern Scotland many years ago, where the longer nights in December are more pronounced than in Connecticut where I grew up. When darkness arrives for tea at 3:30 PM and stays until 9 AM, there is a natural feeling of in breath. I would huddle before a coal fire, sometimes alone, sometimes with friends, listening to the rain and wind blustering about outside while I stayed warm and quiet inside. It inspired me to breathe in and sit with myself—a time of reflection and stillness when the world sleeps, and I slow down. This inward stillness contrasted sharply with the summer liveliness which called me outside and into activity late into the bright night of the long day.

After returning to the United States, getting married and starting a family, our celebrations were of course centered around our children. The dark stillness in our house was not so still. Our solstice celebration took place with friends who lived in the hills and had a 40-foot yurt in which was laid a pine bough spiral. At the beginning of the ceremony, the sole illumination was one lit candle standing in the center of the spiral, a reminder that even in the darkness there is always the One Light. Beginning with the youngest child, we each walked the spiral alone to the center to light our own candle. As we returned around the spiral, we carried our candle, bringing the light back out to our community, placing our candle somewhere along the spiral, illuminating it increasingly as we progressed from youngest to eldest. There is magic in such practices, the youngest one bravely and quietly walking along the dark spiral to the center to light the first candle and bring the light back out to the world, accompanied by our surrounding voices lifted in song—alone but supported by community. This particular yurt had a skylight at the top which would reflect the candle's lights below it, looking like a celestial response to our small lights below, a galaxy of divine sparks, the heart glow of community. Such rituals are done all over the world on the longest night, as the darkness is vanquished and the light returns. Magical indeed.

Christmas was, and still is, more complicated. With the commercial emphasis on Christmas beginning often before Halloween, it is easy to become overwhelmed and a little jaded by commercial excess not to mention the pounding of pop Christmas songs in the stores. There is a pressure put on gift buying that misses the point of this sacred holiday that celebrates the birth of the Christ—for me, the birth of the Christ within the heart of each of us.

But Christmas is also a time of magic, the magic of transforming our homes into sparkling wells of lights and color, of sharing love and the joy of being together, of taking on the mantle of Santa Claus bringing gifts to each other. It is a time set aside to remember that we are all sparks of Love walking the planet. It is a time of thinking of others and seeking ways to gift those in need. It is the season of Santa Claus, the jolly old elf who brings gifts and joy and ho ho ho's. In our house, Santa is honored as a living presence who spreads the magic of hope and giving through our own hands and hearts.

We begin our Christmas celebration, sometimes before decorating has begun, with our favorite Christmas movie, Charles Dicken's *A Christmas Carol* (aka *Scrooge*). The story of a dark and tortured man who, with the aid of three spirits, finds his way towards transformation and rebirth has always been a staple of our family celebration. I believe we have at least 10 versions of it, and we must watch all of them. (There are at least 32 films based on this story, including old black and white versions, musical versions, a Muppets version, Disney versions, animated versions, even a one-man version done by Patrick Stewart.)

Each one is a little different, but what all of them do is show us Ebenezer Scrooge, a dark blot on humanity, moving alone through his world spreading negative vibes of depression and hate, making people wilt and shy away from him. This man who was shut off from everything beautiful, deep into his own dark world of isolation and anger, was shown the way through his past life choices to the present and probably unpleasant future. This led him into a new choice, from a selfish material focus on the accumulation of wealth to one of valuing others and a

34

recognition of his own capacity to love and to care for their wellbeing. He was given a good hard look at himself, and simultaneously at the joy and love shared by others around him from which he excluded himself. Thus inspired to change (admittedly through a certain amount of terror, but hey, let's not quibble about the methods of spirits), Scrooge's heart opens and he sees his world through fresh eyes, full of the joy of life, with loving generosity and caring for others. It is not unlike walking the dark spiral to the light at the center and bringing that inner light back out to share with his world.

Any story of transformation is inspiring, but this one, being centered around the spirit of Christmas, highlights those qualities that the Christ brought closer to our hearts. Qualities of love, of joy in life, of giving and caring for all of humanity, of being a source of Light for all the world. If one man can lift himself out of the darkness within, anyone can. And for each person lost in their inner darkness who is brought back into the Light that is his or her birthright, the whole world is brightened.

This is why when Christmas comes, in our house the music comes out, the lights and colors are decking the halls, and we lift our hearts in joyful celebration of the life and beauty of our world, of people caring for each other, of community, of family that is humanity. This is a deeply spiritual holiday for me, one that sings out the possibility for renewal and hope, for joy and peace on earth, and excludes no one. It is a celebration of the deep prayer, "Let there be peace on earth and good will toward all peoples." And true to the nature of our family, it is also a celebration of fun, joy and laughter, for included in our collection of Christmas Carol movies are some that are spoofs of a treasured Spangler tradition—nothing is too sacred for a good laugh.

So from my hearth to yours, may laughter and joy, love and renewal grace your home this holiday. May the transformation that is always imminent open your heart to a greater love that is there within you. And may the growing light fill your eyes with visions of beauty and hope for the future. The light is ours to bring out, the love is ours to give, and the laughter is ours to delight in. May this season of Light warm and renew your heart.

Cycle of Beauty
Susan Beal
November 2017

Fall is the time of year when gardeners hurry to put their gardens to bed, cleaning up after the mess left by killing frosts—blackened stems, shriveled flowers, unripe squashes and tomatoes rotting on the vine, tender leaves and stems reduced to mush. Birds congregate in the trees before heading south in noisy flocks, taking their songs with them. It's the Persephone time of year, when the lovely daughter of Demeter, goddess of agriculture, descends into the underworld, leaving her grief-stricken mother to lament her loss by withdrawing warmth and color from the landscape and plunging the world from summer into winter.

I have been a gardener for many years, and without fail, I dread the coming of the first frost. It looms for weeks, a countdown clock that determines the end of flowers, tender vegetables and herbs, not just in my garden, but in the fields and woods where I gather medicinal plants and wild greens. I struggle with a feeling of melancholy as all but the hardiest plants shrivel and die, and shadows lengthen as the days grow shorter and colder. Where I live, winter lasts for nearly half the year. While winter has its own great beauty, it's hard to let go of the easy, abundant, effortless beauty of the warmer seasons. It takes some time to adjust.

But before winter settles in for good, there's foliage season, the fleeting week or two when the woods and mountains blaze with the colors of sunset. It's the last hurrah of summer, a grand finale of red, orange, and gold to tide us over for the long, cold, monochromatic winter that follows. Foliage season peaks and fades within a week, maybe two, and like a bouquet of brilliant flowers, it is all the more precious for being so short.

It's also the time when thousands of people take trips to view the foliage. Locals call the leaf season tourists "leaf peepers," and towns and villages in Vermont prepare to be deluged with out-of-town visitors arriving to see the fall colors. It's a delightful, uncommercial kind of tourism, based purely on the love and appreciation of beauty. There are no guarantees for a good show, and no certainty about when, exactly, the colors will peak. Many a tourist has booked a foliage tour months in advance only to arrive before the leaves have turned or after they've been stripped from branches by wind or rain. But perhaps that unpredictability and uncertainty is part of the allure, intensifying the excitement and gratitude when the colors are particularly breathtaking, transforming it from a commodity into a blessing.

I've come to believe—no, to experience—that beauty is a vital nutrient. Far from a frill or elitist fancy, beauty is vital to our spirits.

In his book, *Beauty: The Invisible Embrace* (Harper Perrenial, 2005), the late Irish poet, John O'Donahue, describes how the human soul is hungry for beauty and that people seek it everywhere. He goes on to say, "We feel most alive in the presence of the Beautiful, for it meets the needs of our soul."

The beauty of the fall foliage season is brief and lavish—countless millions of leaves of startling vibrancy, fluttering on twigs, swirling through the sky, scudding and drifting across the ground and finally, carpeting lawns and forest floors with the afterglow of foliage season. The bonus to all this beauty is that the thick mulch of leaves protects buried roots and enriches the fertility of the soil as the leaves decompose. Bright foliage and dark soil are beauty in different forms.

We live in a challenging time, forced to cope with over-awareness of all that is ugly and wrong within the world. Like Demeter, we react with grief and rage, unthinkingly burdening and blighting the landscape with our emotions. When the news is as dire as a killing frost and stress drains all color from our view of the world, beauty—like joy—can seem to have disappeared. What's more, it can seem impractical at best, and elitist at worst. Who has time for non-essentials? How dare we cultivate delight in the face of suffering?

But beauty, if we are to learn from Demeter and Hades, is an essential nutrient for the good of the world and a unifier between light and dark. To quote German philosopher Hans-Georg Gadamer, "the experience of the beautiful ... is the invocation of a potentially whole and holy order of things, wherever it may be." (*The Relevance of the Beautiful and Other Essays*, Cambridge University Press, 1998)

Beauty, as it's said, is in the eye of the beholder. Some beauty is obvious, like autumn leaves, while some beauty is hidden, waiting for gratitude or wonder to open our eyes to its presence. I like to imagine that the joy we feel in the glory of fall foliage is captured, like sunlight, by those same leaves and that it trickles deep into the soil as the leaves decompose, like beautiful Persephone descending below ground, bringing her love and beauty to the underworld. Demeter may be keening in grief while Persephone is hidden from her but Hades, in his dark realm, is filled with joy.

Chapter 2: Into the Subtle

Piercing the Veil
Drena Griffith
March 2019

Growing up in the subtropical Coastal South, sun and sea filled my childhood with warmth and reflection. Curious and introspective, I spent many sunny afternoons after school sky-gazing. Though I wouldn't have been able to describe it easily then, there was something magical about the elements and celestial bodies coming together—sky and sun and endless miles of water connecting, flowing, swirling around great unseen edges

This playground of my childhood inspired my first explorations of the inner planes

One afternoon when I was ten years old, I decided rather spontaneously to go sky-gazing to find God's "house." But I wasn't looking for the Jesus of the Gospels recited at Mass and discussed in Sunday School. What appealed to me more was the Old Testament story of God's creation of the world. Even then, I had a love of ritual and structure—and God was certainly thorough and ceremonial as He painstakingly separated darkness from light, air from sea and earth from heaven, then breathed life into animals and human beings

But where was God *before* the six days? Was He alone in a vast void of nothingness?! Surely, He was still out there, up there—back there—waiting to be found before going through all the trouble to make the world and I was going to uncover His hideout!

Slowly, painstakingly, I peeled back the days of creation, layer by layer, looking for the place where God lived before He formed Universe

Clearly, time was a slippery concept for me to grasp because the idea of God waiting in dark pre-Creation silence seemed quite tangible in my mind's eye. Even so, though I'd like to say that I discovered the Source inspiring such sincere devotion, most days I returned empty-handed, with throbbing temples. But that rarely slowed me down! For many years I played a game of hide and seek with the Infinite

In my early thirties, after one too many life disappointments and on the edge of leaving Christianity, I wrote the following poem about that early experience:

"As a child I believed in the orderliness of God more so than in his goodness; I watched as the sky twisted itself from light to dark, from shape to void; that's where God lives, I told myself, before he formed universe

My child's mind never thought to look for God inside my young life; he existed beyond the repugnancy of dawn and sunsets; outside of storm and insomniac dreams. Outside of time, where matter had not yet been forced into cruel shapes, it didn't matter what love was and where it could not be found no matter how hard I concentrated my focus

With my childhood sky I had an Infinity that had not yet taken on names. With my childhood faith I had God unstaged."

Now, more than three decades after my childhood vigil, and extensive exposure to a number of diverse spiritual approaches, including Incarnational Spirituality, I see those childhood efforts in a brighter light. They were my first attempt at piercing the veil, peering into the unseen realms that Lorian and others refer to as the subtle worlds. Now, it's hard for me to not feel appreciation and respect towards an early recognition of what so many people find mysterious and invisible

But of course now I also know we can do more than gaze longingly across the chasm. Surely, we can visit those realms and interact within them as easily as we can our neighborhoods, communities, and childhood playgrounds. In fact, more and more scientific research, including a recent experiment in creating and measuring "objective reality" ("A quantum experiment suggests there's no such thing as objective reality," by Emerging Technology from the arXiv, *MIT Technology Review*, March 2019) lends credence to the possibility that what we consider the known, visible world may actually depend upon the vision of the beholder — something that mystics and children have known for eons.

As I have progressed on my own spiritual journey, my connection with the subtle worlds remains curiously similar to my early voyages. Though I no longer see God living in a house outside of time, or see myself as separate from Divinity, it's still enjoyable to gaze lovingly into the subtle skies from time to time, hoping to discover a fresh sighting of an old Friend.

Questions: Head or Heart
Claire Blatchford
July 2019

As I wrote about a month ago, following questions is one of the great challenges, pleasures and wonders of my life. And over the years I've observed how different the questions that originate in my head can be from those that arise in my heart. The former are usually more probing, figure-it-out, get-on-with-what's-at-hand, or curiosity questions. The latter are more open ended, receptive, invitational, empathic. This is not to say all my questions are either one or the other—as if only from head or from heart. The two often arise out of or blend into each other, even as thoughts can arise out of feelings or feelings out of thoughts. And the two may, at times, be so finely interwoven I don't regard them as primarily one or the other.

I'm mentioning these two types of questions because both arise within me. They're *my* questions, not yours, though they might echo or supplement what you're saying. You likely can hear in the way they're phrased, my intent, personal opinion, emotional stance and sense of sovereignty. My husband sometimes responds with, "Hey, that's a loaded question!" Or "What do you mean, *really*? Can you please say that a bit more clearly?"

There are also questions I hear—these are the ones I've been pondering recently—that come from more mysterious places, not from my own mind or heart. They nudge or invite me into a more alert—or even a more relaxed—mode of attentiveness. More alert in that I'm aware when I hear them something is going on just beyond the reach of my physical senses and I need to pay attention. More relaxed in that I know I need to slow down and step back from life-as-usual into a condition of friendly openness and receptivity to whatever, or whomever, is speaking through the question I'm hearing.

Being with young children who are full of questions has always been, for me, a helpful way of shaping both the more alert and more relaxed forms of attentiveness. Especially children who are not yet reading the printed word and are busy trying to absorb the writing of the life in which they're immersed. Here are some questions I remember hearing:

"*How* are they attached?" our eldest daughter wanted to know, and rather urgently, in the middle of a display of fireworks when she was four.

When I told our younger daughter around that same age one Monday morning that her father had gone away for a couple of days she asked when he'd be back.

"Friday," was my response.

Off she went to play, returning ten minutes later to ask, "*Is* it Friday?"

I remember our eldest granddaughter in the aviary at the Washington D.C. zoo earnestly asking, "Am I growing wings?"

And yet another question, from another granddaughter to her mother early one morning, "Are you *in* my dream?"

Questions like these intrigue and delight because there's an unexpected freshness to them which jiggles our way of looking at the world. It's as though the child is not yet fully here, in incarnation, may still be connected to the subtle realms from which she came and, therefore, more alert to the subtle realms in which she's landed. I've always heard these questions as a request to stay open to a wonder-filled and magical way of being in our world. Aren't fireworks attached to our imaginative powers? Isn't time timeless when we love someone and are with them or wish to be with them? Aren't we in each other's dreams? Can you too feel yourself becoming bird when absorbed in watching bird flight?

Later, after a child's change of teeth and the start of elementary school, I've gotten some pretty pointed questions asking for the same alert or relaxed response:

"Why is he (the homeless man begging on the road divider) texting on a cell phone?"

"What *is* multitasking? How do I do that?"

To me: "Why do you like dancing so much if you're deaf?"

Also to me: "Do *you* ever dream of *your* grandma and grandpa?"

In addition to questions from children, I've sensed animals, many of whom seem to be endlessly curious about us, asking questions too. Take the questions in the eyes of our dogs beginning with the plaintive, "Why can't I go with you?" to "Do you *know* what you're doing?" (No question about it, I sometimes *don't* know what I'm doing.)

Then there are questions I hear within myself, absent any visible

43

outer form of being. You might say they come to you "out of the blue." An example of this happened years ago one Easter in the middle of a luncheon at my parent's home. My mother turned to me at the exact same moment I turned to her and asked the exact same question I was about to ask her: "How is Annabelle?"

Annabelle had done housework in the past for my maternal grandmother and my mother. She was then retired and lived an hour away from my parents but maybe fifteen minutes from us, so it made sense my mother asked me about her. And I, though I hadn't seen her for a couple of years, there was Annabelle on the tips of our tongues!

To shorten the story, I promised my mother I would check on Annabelle the next morning. I found her alone and in a disoriented condition. I promised to visit her the next day too, but she died that very night.

To this day it's my understanding the question of Annabelle's well-being came to both my mother and to me because she needed to be on her way, yet also needed to be remembered, reassured, perhaps even given permission to make her exit. Who was asking the question? Annabelle's soul? An angel? One of her subtle allies? I don't know but am glad my mother and I were able to hear and act on it.

Let me give one more example of hearing a question within myself and feeling compelled then also to act in response to it. On this occasion I was awoken about 2:30 am by a voice, "Is your writing finished?" At that time, I'd been working on a book for several months and had had a not very productive day. I was in no mood to get up and return to my desk. I was about to drift back to sleep when the question returned, quite a bit louder, "**IS** your writing finished?"

Now, fully awake, I sat up certain the voice was John's voice. And it was the sort of question he'd ask. John, a close friend and mentor had for years been interested in my writing and had often offered discerning editorial suggestions. He'd died several years before. I knew the book I was then working on was on a topic he'd been involved in at the time of his passing.

I got up, went to my computer and switched it on. I reread what I'd written to see if, by chance, it was indeed finished. It didn't sound finished. In fact, it sounded pretty muddled. As I sat there hoping the question that had prompted me to get up might point to a better way to express my thoughts, the red flag on my email icon popped up. Curious to know who might be emailing at 3 in the morning I clicked on and found a message from Kathy.

Kathy had graduated over 25 years earlier from the high school John was heading at that time. She also been awoken by John. Not by a question heard within but by her wish that he was still alive and she could talk with him. That was what she wanted to tell me. We'd exchanged many handwritten letters and emails in the past but, right then, hadn't been in touch for over a year.

The thought that we both—several, hundred miles apart yet in the same time zone-- had been awoken at the same hour in some way by John gave me goose bumps.

This is giving me chills!" Kathy typed after I told her I was certain the question that had gotten me up was from him. "Me too!" I wrote back, as another round of goose bumps came on.

Then I asked, because I could still hear John voice, and felt in my heart he wanted me to keep on writing, not on my book but with her, "How are you?" We typed back and forth for about an hour online.

Not all the questions I hear within—and listen to and respond to—lead to such dramatic synchronic moments, but it's happened often enough for me to want to be ready to follow the next one that comes along.

The Art and Craft of Collaborative Fields
Freya Secrest
July 2017

The subject of "collaborative fields" came up recently in a conversation I had with Mary Inglis, a facilitator of the Game of Transformation. Mary defined a collaborative field as a particular ecology of relationship in which one consciously takes steps to foster a whole that is greater than the sum of its parts. She described some of the steps they use in the Game process which helps to lead to such a field: "We always start a game with attunement—to ourselves, to each other, to our activity and purpose. We also consciously invite in the "Game Deva", that overarching presence that works with the game process." She further outlined that each game is guided by a stated intention that helps to focus the group effort by connecting the participants with a common purpose.

These are important group building processes, but I wondered what is the "magic" or "zing" that ignites attunement and shared purpose into a new wholeness? That seems harder to pin down. Mary used the results of her experiences in the Game to point to possibilities: "You know how sometimes you look at what you have been doing and you see it is more than you thought it was? This happens in a game when we have created a collaborative field." She pointed to the magic that leads to a new wholeness as emerging out of the attitude each person held and brought to their participation in a game. In her work she noticed that the willingness of participants to engage all parts of themselves, energetic, physical, mental, emotion, subtle, spirit and soul made a difference. It was when each person brought their full selves forward with commitment to the ecology of the process that new "whole-making" would most often happen.

I was intrigued by the thought that I might nurture a similar collaborative field in my own daily life and activities and curious about how to foster and encourage its development. I did not want to just wait and hope it would "happen." First, in considering my own experiences, I began by looking at the moments when I noticed synchronicities or connections with others or the world around. Those are my first thoughts of a collaborative energy at work. What I noticed about the synchronicities is that they can happen at a meeting or around a shared creative project, and sometimes even when I am alone in a reflective, quiet state where an answer or idea that solves some daily issue pops to mind. Upon further reflection, I realized that at those times I am in a loving state, not a head-over-heels "in love" but a resilient, at-peace and "in tune" loving. In that state of love, I generate an energy or "field" of connectedness within myself that flows out and links with the world around me.

Magic Step #1: Love is the foundation for a collaborative field.

This loving state needs a place where it can land and grow. My reflections jumped to the interaction of the Four Incarnational Principles of Identity (Standing), Boundary (Holding), Relationship (Energizing), and Emergence (Co-Creating). Each of these ideas hold a different signature or element of connection for me and together they shape a balanced place where I engage, integrate and grow through my life events. Going back to Mary's definition of collaborative fields as attunement to ourselves, to each other, to the subtle ecology of life and to our activity and purpose, it is through being able to bring my love into the diversity of my everyday life that I bring about the possibility of new "wholeness".

Magic step #2: Engaging in our own life and incarnation is the place where collaborative wholeness can root and grow.

Coming to appreciate the different essences of the Four Incarnational Principles has been a process that is evolving for me. Using these principles helps me to better understand the magical wholeness that emerges out of my life. But I can't do it only from the level of thinking or even feeling; I must embody these qualities with a physical stance or action that encapsulates their energy.

Sovereignty fits with the uprightness of standing, connected through head and feet to the stars and earth, and through my skin with the world around. So I often physically stand to create a link to this element.

Boundary creates a place of connection where differences meet—a lap that can hold or arms that encircle and define the space of inside and outside. When I sit or hold something I link with the energy of boundary by the very shape I take.

Relationship I see as an activity of exchange where differences can meet "eye to eye" with respect and recognition of the value of self and other. When I look at someone or something I try to bring that attitude of respect into my gaze and approach to our relationship.

The idea of Emergence has evolved in me to be the stance of the open hand. It requires a strong energy of standing and balance in order to hold an openness to the other. It is something I try to explore through developing my capacity for invitation and welcome.

Although each principle is involved with the others, it is emergence that is particularly connected to the idea of collaborative fields for me because it is a place where we discover and are surprised by newness. What fosters emergence is that sense of loving invitation—the open hand. I imagine I am offering a treat to a shy deer and feel how still, strong, and at peace I need to be in myself to give the other "room" to come forward. When this is hard, it is usually because I am turned inward, closely focused in my own life. But when I turn toward the life around me in the spirit of love, welcome, and open-handedness, then my energy and imagination can begin to foster collaborative possibilities. This to me is the art and the craft of a collaborative field.

Have You heard an Inner Voice Lately?
Julia Spangler
May 2019

Throughout human history, mystics and gifted teachers have emerged in every culture, expanding our understanding of what it means to be human. We are not simply physical bodies brought to life by an accident of evolution. There is a deeper experience of being human than just thought and emotion that includes our capacity to an expanded awareness of non-physical realities.

It is notable that today in our world, non-physical elements are being talked about more openly—what we in Lorian call subtle worlds and subtle beings. They are not new. The subtle worlds have been around and making themselves known throughout time. Ancient books tell stories of encounters with angelic beings. Inspiration and direction from inner sources have always been freely spoken of by religious and spiritual leaders. And I have heard many stories from individuals who have had experiences at one time or other of being nudged from within to do something or go somewhere. We call these perceptions subtle for a reason. We cannot see any particular cause for the feeling, so we may tend to dismiss it as being unreal. But it is my contention that everyone has these subtle experiences, whether or not they pay attention or give them credence.

In my own experience, I have several times heard an inner voice telling me something I needed to know. The first time was when I was a teenager listening to some family members who were discussing spiritual things. I wondered why I wasn't joining in, since I felt drawn to the subject, when I heard a voice telling me that it wasn't time. I knew this voice was right, with a kind of inner knowing that was familiar and peaceful and sure. I knew also that I would know when and where the time was right—and I did, when I turned 20. A strong inner nudge launched me off to Findhorn, a spiritual community in Northern Scotland, to begin my spiritual education. How did I know it was time? Well, it is subtle! I felt like a door opened that hadn't been there before.

These inner voices may inspire disbelief in us. Are we really hearing someone? Am I imagining this? It can be hard to determine sometimes. We are not usually trained to trust our inner nudges. Some years ago,

David and I happened to drop in on our friends Fritz and Vivienne Hull just as they were finishing up a week-long meditation retreat at the Chinook Learning Center on Whidbey Island. Fritz grabbed us and said, "Come here, I have to show you something!" as he took us across the meadow to where some of the participants had camped during the week. As we walked, he told us an extraordinary story. One of the women in the group had awakened in the night feeling uneasy. She felt like she had to get up and move.

As she lay in her tent in the dark trying to decide if she wanted to leave her warm sleeping bag and go out into the cold night, she heard a loud voice say with compelling urgency, "Get out and run left!" She immediately scrambled out of her tent and went left just as a tree in the forest near where she was camped cracked. The top third of this tall tree speared through her tent and right through her sleeping bag! Just as Fritz finished his story, we turned in to the camping meadow and saw what he was describing. It looked like a huge, sharpened spear was standing upright in the ground pierced right through the heart of this tent. It must have been about 15 feet tall! The remainder of the splintered tree, about 25 more feet, stood on the edge of the forest nearby. This was a breathtaking and disturbing sight!

But what was this voice she heard? What was the voice I heard in my teens? Is it part of ourselves that perceives beyond the range of our usual senses? Or is it another presence that is giving us aid? Many people have these extraordinary experiences and cannot deny that there are unseen presences which can communicate with us unexpectedly. So how about intentionally? Can we communicate with subtle realms at will?

Some can. My friend, and co-founder of Findhorn, Dorothy Maclean did. She did not hear voices as some do, but could connect during her meditations with bright, angelic, radiant intelligences which she called Devas (the term "angel" had too many religious connotations for her comfort!). She received impressions from the Devas that she would put into her own words. What she learned through these communications was always new to her, things she would not herself have thought. I saw evidence of this when I was traveling with her once. We had stopped in a California redwood grove off of Highway 101 which, according to the plaque near the grove, was being preserved for posterity. We could see that the trees in the grove were dying. Dorothy felt overcome with grief over the toll that human development was taking on the redwood forests. She took some time while we were there to meditate and communicate with the Deva of the Redwoods. She found herself apologizing for the damage that humans were doing to the trees. The response she got was a surprise to her. She wrote this message down:

"Small mortal and great being, we greet you. Come with us, up high above the traffic noise ... to where everlasting peace is. Let the 'evil' be as dust on your feet, to be shaken off and returned to itself, while the peace of God remains, the creative peace which cloaks a planet and many forms of life.

What if the trees come toppling down? Their vibrations are forever part of life here and we are glad to have contributed as much as we have. Rejoice, for life moves on, whatever form it takes—and it is one life, as we well know. We are part of you, you are part of us, and so it will always be."

To the Deva consciousness, everything is an expression of spirit and if it was time for the form of the redwood to pass out of the world, there would be another form for its essence to take. The shape of the form did not matter. For Dorothy, this was a reminder that the perspective of the devic realm was not human in any way but always offered a bigger picture. For me, it was a reminder that collaboration with inner beings can offer us a shift in perspective, a broadening and deepening of how we see our world.

There is a deeper experience of being human that includes our capacity to connect with the unseen part of the world. It is a natural part of who we are though, as I have said, often a discounted one. It is too easy to dismiss those delicate whispers of intuition that get submerged in the everyday din of our ordinary reality. If we take time to give attention to these inner nudges, to give them a little more weight and recognition, we might find ourselves beginning to come more easily into connection with the subtle worlds. And if those inner nudges become a loud shout, we might want to move on it!

The Inner Voice
Claire Blatchford
March 2016

"Inner hearing" has always been crucial in my life—particularly as I'm deaf and can't always manage by way of a hearing aid (used for over 50 years) and now, more recently, a cochlear implant. When I share this conviction people often ask, "Can one hear and converse with spiritual beings in the same way one hears and converses with people?" My response is "Yes!" But I think it's important to realize conversing with spiritual or subtle beings, as with human beings, occurs in many ways and on many levels, not just in words as we know them. Inner hearing or "inner knowing", which may be the better term, differs in my own experiences from "outer hearing" or hearing things in the physical world in two ways.

First, what I hear within is not specifically and only about hearing non-physical beings. I might, for example, hear suddenly and unexpectedly into the thoughts, concerns or joys of someone I'm close to who is far away and has not made an attempt to contact me by phone or email. This could also be called intuitive hearing and leads directly to my second point: inner hearing engages me in a deeper and more comprehensive way than ordinary physical hearing.

When I hear the world by way of physical hearing, with the aid of my implant, it's usually in a cause-and-effect way. Our dog barks and I deduce from his bark someone is at the back door. When I hear inwardly, the physical and emotional feelings that accompany this form of hearing are as much the message as the thought that's being expressed. Also, when I hear within I may at the same time be hearing the outer world by way of the cochlear implant. It's not as though I only hear one way or the other. I'm sure this happens to people with normal hearing all the time, like when the phone rings and even before you've picked it up you intuitively know who is calling.

What I have to share about my discovery of inner hearing as a child may help to illustrate these two points.

I first heard *inwardly* when I was six (shortly after becoming profoundly deaf in both ears overnight from the mumps). I didn't get my first hearing aid until I was twelve, as there weren't any aids at that time powerful enough for my use. So I was cut off during those years from the usual things children hear with their ears. I'm certain I became aware of inner hearing because I was removed from the clamor of everyday noises.

At the same time, I never thought of myself as living in a silent world because I'd known what hearing was and because what I "heard" through my eyes—people talking and showing facially how they felt, cars driving by, dogs barking, waves breaking on the beach—translated into inner sounds. Yet I obviously couldn't hear and talk in the usual ways. Ordinary communication—hearing, understanding what I heard, and speaking—was extremely difficult. When you can't hear, you can't moderate your own voice and your speech can get sloppy pretty quickly. So it was marvelous indeed when, without any, "WHAT did you say?" or "For Pete's sakes repeat that!" I heard an inner voice without stress or struggle.

I can't remember the first time I heard it. In some mysterious way I assumed it had always been there, which, in turn, led me to assume everyone heard their own inner voice. When I was twelve and told my best friend about it she said maybe the Devil was talking to me. The thought had never occurred to me. As I felt helped and comforted by the inner voice, never bullied or threatened, I didn't take her words seriously and didn't speak of inner hearing with anyone again until I was in my twenties.

The inner voice was direct, simple and supportive. It was never ostentatious or effusive. I never questioned or tried to shield myself from it because it always "got" me and exactly where I needed to be met, held, or corrected. As in:

"You're okay." When I wondered if I was "normal" and not "stupid" or "dumb", as in "deaf and dumb", the saying used at that time. (I was the only deaf kid in my school district.)

"Cool it!" When I was angry at perceived unfairness towards myself or others. The tone by itself could literally pop my hot air balloon and bring me back to earth. I also discovered how words spoken in anger could boomerang right back, wounding me. In this manner I learned there are other angles, besides my own, in every situation.

The words I heard were, at times, like arrows in that I was immediately struck by the truth of what was being said. Not wounding arrows, but arrows that hit the bullseye, showing me an inner kernel of truth in situations I found myself in.

What I heard within was never felt as *command* but always as *loving suggestion*. "Go home and help your mother" was one I heard more than once. The suggestions were so clear, so obviously right, it was as though what I heard flowed right into inner consent, then out in actions. And there was always space for me to hear or not hear, accept or reject what was being said. I could, if I wanted, go right on being angry and feeling sorry for myself. There were no veiled threats of likely punishment from the inner voice. I did find, though, that when I liked the drama of being angry and feeling sorry for myself, I was often unable to hear the inner voice very clearly, if at all.

Whose was the voice I was hearing? I never thought to ask. It knew me and I knew it: that was enough. Julia Spangler expressed her response to her inner voice beautifully:

"What is important to me is that I knew without a doubt that the voice was real. I felt like it knew something I didn't, and it was right. I didn't need to ask if it was real. I knew it was for me, and I knew I could trust it. How did I know? I suppose in the same way I know when I can trust a person. There is a comfort and feeling of rightness to the relationship. And then, experience through my life teaches me if it is right."

Connecting with this inner voice at six brought me to the conviction I live with now sixty-six years later: inner beings are eagerly waiting for us to hear them and to acknowledge their presence. Their hope is that we might together find our way into a new understanding of the interconnectedness of the seen and unseen, the human and the earthly, the physical and the subtle aspects of all life. In fact, I believe all life depends on our connecting in this way. This, from my perspective, is what Incarnational Spirituality is all about.

Being in Love
Mary Reddy
September 2019

An open heart. For me, this was a long time coming. For me, this is an active, continuing endeavor. A grail long sought has begun to show me its shining presence. I am awed by the power that beats in the heart of love.

I know people who love me but whose hearts are well defended. Perhaps the love is no less, but without vulnerability, its power to transform is diminished. I did not see this as a lack until I began to open my heart. In truth, I instinctively valued the shallow plane of exchange we allotted each other, those of us who were afraid of opening more. I am finding new ways to love, stepping gingerly outside my fortress walls while honoring others' need for remaining within.

When I want to conjure the power and vulnerability of love, I see my children. My love for them is fierce, though it has often reached them imperfectly, twisting past my fortress walls. Even when this mother love remained stuck within me, I still felt its vulnerability keenly. The possibility of grief yawns beneath the joy of sharing our lives together. I had learned well the lessons of my culture and my childhood—better not go into that vulnerable place. Don't borrow trouble.

How do we resolve this instinct for self-protection with our desire to open to love? Not just in our personal lives but especially when considering subtle activism in this world of increasing hatred, violence, and natural disasters? Years ago, I learned a subtle healing technique from my shaman teacher. I found it difficult and have not practiced it often so I may not relate the steps as accurately as he would. It involves journeying to your allies, perhaps to a special ally who partners with you in healing endeavors. You request this ally's protection and assistance. You fill yourself up with love and light and you journey shamanically to the site of a disaster to offer this light to the victims. You are to see the light pouring from portals in your wrists and hands. Those in need will come to you and feed on the light. The idea is to channel this love and light with the assistance of your ally, not to provide it from your own self for the demand will deplete you.

I remember I performed this exercise right after Hurricane Katrina swept through New Orleans. Tuning in, I saw a grey swath swirling over the surface of the water-logged land, filled with hundreds of suddenly dead people. I reached out my arms and invited them to come feed on me. Shocked, bereft, or aggrieved, they swarmed toward me. I felt a number of them fill up and become released. But eventually I felt I needed to end my journey. I left reluctantly because I saw so many more I had not yet tended to. Of course, they would not remain untended; a number of angels and helpers were probably on hand to help these souls transition. What struck me most after completing this practice was the way it aroused my own fear of loss and death. Not a place of strength from which to act! Maybe this approach should be labeled "Expert practitioners only. Do not do this at home." With my fear of vulnerability, I did not feel safe enough to do this again.

Years later, Incarnational Spirituality strengthened my sense of sovereignty and gave me new tools for subtle activism. A first step in subtle activism—or actually in any attempt to connect with subtle beings and energies—is to place myself in the state I wish to share. Love is a great starting point (including self-love). And so, I imagine the love I have for my children. And I begin to sense how this love grows and stretches beyond to all sorts of connections. A deeper vein of this love calls to me now. It is the unwalled courageous heart that carries a full sense of vulnerability.

If we read about the victims of mass shootings, if we imagine the pain and fear of the migrant children separated from those they love and on whom they've depended for survival and support, the well-trained culturally approved reaction is to allow ourselves a brief moment of feeling that pain and horror. Maybe we can hurl our anger at those responsible, but then we must retreat into learned helplessness. A better option is to surge into political action. Another is to connect with our allies, generate love and healing, and in whatever fashion move that loving energy out to those who need it. Doing this, we never know rationally to what extent we've been helpful. And the danger, as I see it, is in a new kind of complacency. Because we've performed subtle activism, we can put the horror of the situation aside and go about our lives.

It gets tricky putting things like this into words. Of course, there is value in going about our lives since every act performed with love generates more good than we can imagine. But I am beginning to see a way to deepen this subtle work in the same way that I deepen my engagement with everyone I love, with every being I meet in my everyday local sphere. Perhaps I can amp up the power in my subtle healing work in the same way that I can increase the power of love in my own life.

Here's a story that may seem like a sidetrack. Once I was vacuuming the rug in the living room of the off-campus apartment I shared with fellow students. The old Hoover began to groan and whir, so I tipped it sideways to see what was stuck. With all the impracticality of my youth, I foolishly stuck my finger into the vacuum hole without turning it off and was struck by some kind of rotating beaters lurking just inside. My finger was smashed and badly cut; the pain almost caused me to faint. Again the foolish youth, I ran to my roommate's liquor stash and swallowed a shot of peach brandy, thinking that would dull the pain. It did not. I went to lie on my bed and as it was hopeless to ignore the pain, I went into it. My awareness moved into the shrieking finger, I merged with the intense pain, and suddenly I felt an intense love for life. Like the continuum between hot and cold, how something can be so hot that it feels like freezing, I could no longer tell what was pain and what was the intense joy of being alive, my deep and wild love of life. I told an acquaintance about this later. I did not know how to put it into words so I simply said I'd hurt so much that I'd seen God. He replied, "Oh boy, you must be a real masochist!" He did not get it. It was not about enjoying pain. I had been mystically transported to the place where pain and love are one. Vacuum cleaners, peach brandy, and transcendence—who knew?

Seriously though, this is a clue to my new direction in subtle work. It's about not walling yourself off from the pain. It looks like this. First, I partner with my allies and step fully into the intense joy of love. I feel it shining through my little toes, shooting out every strand of hair on my head. I feel it sifting into the air about me, washing over and through my environment. And I feel my surroundings returning that love to me. Then I imagine the circumstances of the violence or tragedy I wish to attend to. As best I can, I touch into the full horror, the intense anger, grief, and fear of the people I hope to help. I mustn't shy away from the emotions and shift to a 'higher' plane but feel them simultaneously with that intense love I've conjured. That love is capable of infinite consolation, of tender protection, and soul-and-body-satisfying nurturance. And that love can hold those qualities while also letting in the pain. I can shed tears and know joy at the same time. I imagine the pain and sorrow, all the horror and rage, stepping into the shelter of this great love's cloak.

As with manifestation, this healing for others works to the extent that I embody it in myself. This practice asks me to become vulnerable in my heart while holding fast to an invincible love. I become the cauldron that does not shrink from pain. And amazingly, that great love we all can access holds me safe as I hold, acknowledge, and honor all the feelings. Those suffering pain and loss are not denied their feelings but are invited into the safe holding of love. They can know themselves because they are seen for who they are, in all their pain and longing.

So many things deconstruct the fortress around our hearts: self-love, trust, gratitude, beauty, a child's gleeful laugh, the awareness of the tender vulnerability of others. What blasts the walls down, for me, is being in love enough to feel it all. When I am in love, I no longer need to shy away from the dark.

Excess Baggage
Susan Beal
September 2017

A sense of urgency always overtakes me when I get to an airport, even when I am in plenty of time. It's the overall vibe, I suppose, of a seeming *non-place*—everyone there is rushing off to somewhere else or working to get people from here to there. The muffled, subsonic vibration of jets overhead and the smell of diesel that permeates everything adds to the unsettled feeling. The process of going through airport security adds to the stress.

One day a few years ago, my husband David and I were flying home from Sea-Tac. He had gotten TSA pre-check and I had not. I waved goodbye to him as he sauntered off to his special check-in point—no line there—and I paused to fish my wallet and ID out of my backpack. Just then, a gaggle of Japanese school girls sashayed past, and all at once I was at least 20 people farther back in line than I would have been moments ago. It wasn't a big deal, since we were in plenty of time and it hardly mattered if we waited here or at the gate. But I smoldered as the line barely inched forward. I saw David collect his bags from the conveyor belt, clear of security. It was so unfair!

I told myself I was being silly. Our flight didn't leave for two hours. Everything was fine. Yet everything rankled and my nose was out of joint. What was wrong with me? The morning had started off well. I had just finished the second of four weekends that were part of the Lorian Ordination Program. I had been in a fine—even inspired—mood. And although airport security is tiresome at the best of times, I'm generally laid back. Even if I get upset, I can usually summon a sense of gratitude to lighten up. It's fun to get a hassled security officer to smile, or to share a sense of amusement with fellow passengers at the mild indignities we were all enduring. I also like to recognize and say hello to the life and sentience within the airport building, the monitors and machines, the subtle beings and energies at work alongside their physical counterparts, unseen and rarely acknowledged.

On this occasion, however, I couldn't summon the least smile. To make matters worse, after I'd been in line for fifteen minutes or so, a TSA officer ushered everyone just behind me into a new, shorter line. I escalated from petty annoyance, to robust anger, to simmering rage.

As I looked around me at the mass of people being processed by armed, uniformed officials, my mood shifted into something darker and more troubling. Suddenly, we were not air passengers having our bags checked for bombs and knives, we were refugees being herded into camps, prisoners in a gulag, illegal aliens captured for incarceration and deportation. The scene around me was superimposed in my mind with images of Jews being unloaded from cattle cars and sorted on train platforms, of women in headscarves being harassed by military troops. On top of anger, I was flooded with grief about the cruelty humanity visits upon itself. Clearly these weren't all my own thoughts and feelings, but why was I picking up on them so strongly?

I shook my head. I needed to get a hold of myself. I gazed around me and reoriented to the present. Amidst the hubbub, a woman in the cylindrical x-ray machine raised her arms. A guard ran a beeping scanning baton over a man's pockets. A mother bent down to help her young daughter put a Dora the Explorer bag on the conveyor. Tall, potted ficus trees presided calmly over the crowd. Sunlight filtered down from skylights high up on the ceiling. I could see blue sky through the glass, and clouds drifting past. I breathed in, I breathed out. But I was still mired in anger and grief.

I collected my stuff, put everything back into place, then found David, who was smiling as I approached him. I thought, "Fine for him to smile! He didn't have to wait in line!" We decided to grab lunch before heading to the gate. After we ordered food, I ran through various techniques for grounding and calming myself, but I couldn't regain my equilibrium. Things didn't improve on the plane. We were in the last row, in seats that didn't recline because they were up against the bathroom wall. The smell of bathroom disinfectant wafted over us and the man in the aisle seat crunched noisily through bag after smelly bag of onion-sour cream potato chips.

Finally, somewhere over the middle of the United States, my mood began to lift. Hurtling through space in a winged aluminum cylinder, subjected to bad odors, limited personal space, minimal oxygen, and an accumulation of annoyances, I started to feel better. They say angels can fly because they take themselves lightly. Maybe it works the other way around, too—when you fly, you take yourself more lightly. My mood lightened—not entirely, but I no longer felt hijacked by rage and despair.

Flying always makes me aware of the angelic and elemental beings who assist the material world. It's not just physics that keep planes aloft, but the assistance of angels and sylphs. And the view above the clouds reinforces a sense of celestial collaboration. Also, I find the enforced inactivity of being stuffed into a plane seat conducive to meditation and self-reflection. When I fly, I review my life. What effect it would have if I went down in a plane? How would my family fare? What messes and blessings would I leave behind? It puts things in perspective.

The plane landed, thanks to the human and subtle teamwork. Once home, the peace and familiarity of our land and house embraced me. I sat down to center myself and do some energy work to ground and transmute the psychic gunk that had thrown me off. Despite, or maybe because of my sensitivity, I often don't make a distinction between energies that originate with me and energies that are no more mine than the rain falling from a cloud or the exhaust from a tail pipe.

I reviewed the morning's events from a clairvoyant perspective. I saw the emotional residue of thousands of people's irritation, fear, and frustration accumulating in the check point area, like an ecosystem overburdened with toxic runoff. There were vague shapes moving among the heavy residues, perhaps a combination of projections and thought-forms left behind by travelers and more autonomous beings who find nourishment in such an environment, like rats in a garbage-strewn lot.

I felt stupid and chagrined for having been thrown so far off center. What kind of a Lorian priest would I make? I asked my inner guides for their perspective and all at once I was flooded with a new understanding. I often take on difficult energies from other people and places. I used to feel vulnerable, even victimized by my sensitivity, but I've learned through the years how to cope more effectively and safely with discordant energies. In this case, the subtle cleaning crew at the airport had recognized I had those skills and had handed me a bag of psychic trash to recycle when I got home.

Apparently, I'd agreed to it on a subconscious level. Yes, I'd gotten whammied at first by "leakage" from the bag, but I'd contained it until it could be properly transmuted and my subtle courier services were much appreciated. I smiled as I thought of the constant warnings played over airport PA systems about not accepting bags or packages from any unknown person. Little did the TSA know it was happening all the time in ways they hadn't imagined! Since then, I've learned to be a more conscious — and careful — partner in such work.

Finding My Stance
Claire Blatchford
July 2016

When I've been confused or in distress, Incarnational Spirituality has, many times, offered me a helpful and steadying stance. Not a creed, dogma, or set of rules, but, quite literally, a stance. Stance as defined three ways in the *Merriam Webster Collegiate Dictionary*: "a) a way of standing or being placed, b) an intellectual or emotional attitude, c) the position of both body and feet from which an athlete starts or operates."

I like the word stance and these three definitions because Incarnational Spirituality is definitely, for me, a way of standing or being placed, not only on this earth but within the specific incarnation I'm in now. This earth, the natural world, the invisible world I can sense within this world, family, friends, and various communities I'm connected to, the time in history I've incarnated into: stance implies relationship with all of these things. When I feel I'm standing in relationship with one, the other, or all of them—rather than ignoring, condemning, retreating or hiding from them—I know I'm not alone. (This is not to say there aren't times when I need to retreat, rest, and lie low, in order to gather strength to stand again.) I can also sense there are deep meanings behind all these connections, meanings I may not yet be fully aware of, meanings that wait to be discovered, explored, and worked with.

I also know when I'm standing straight with ease and strength because I feel clear and able, and I mean this not just physically but intellectually and emotionally. And I know when I'm not straight intellectually and emotionally, am wobbly, weighed down, or hunched over with worries, uncertainties, fears, and so on. Likewise, when I am standing straight, there's an invigorating, athletic feel to it. The feel of, "I can go for it! I can find my way into and through it." Be it a difficult or unhappy situation or even a super busy or grey day. In short, it's the stance of feeling empowered because I've chosen to be an incarnated human being at this time within a certain web of relationships.

I recently, to my own amazement, found the reassurance and power of this stance in my dream life; it is there within me when I'm asleep as well as when I'm awake. Here is the dream that alerted me to this:

I dreamt I was lost in a strange city. I was standing on the sidewalk bare foot with only the clothes on my back. No car, no keys, no wallet, identification cards, money, known address to return to or destination to go to. No cell phone. No familiar faces passing by. No eye contact with any of these obviously very busy, very purpose- filled passersby.

I am, by the way, a country girl, not a city girl. In the country I often see places—within a thicket, beside a stream, beneath an old tree—where I know I could pause and find my bearings if I wasn't sure of the way. But not in the midst of a city. Because of this I was (in the dream) flooded with momentary panic: Where was I? Where was I supposed to be going? Curiously I was most upset not by the loss of all forms of identification or currency but by the absence of my eyeglasses. How was I going to read a train schedule, a map, a newspaper? How was I going to find, and make sense of, whatever I might be directed to?

Then a wave of something warm washed over me, not just once but several times, and I knew one thing for sure: I was standing upright on my feet. My own two feet that have carried me upstairs and down, up mountains and down, everywhere from dawn to dusk, day after day since I first stood up, through every situation— easy or hard—I've been through thus far. And, though I wasn't wearing shoes, my feet weren't the least bit cold, like the cold feet I've been getting the last four or five years. So cold I need to wear socks when I go to bed.

I looked up and saw deep blue, cloudless sky overhead. I didn't know what city I was in, didn't know where I was supposed to go, or if people spoke in English or a foreign language, but there was the sky. The thought that the sky belongs to everyone, no matter where one is, has always been important to me. My heart rose as it always does when greeting clear sky expanse and openness. And there was the sun. That, to me, meant the stars were there in the sky also, though, as usual, not visible during the daylight hours. I felt steadied.

Looking down I saw the earth. Pavement, pebbles, dirt, bits of twigs from a tree, and, to my right, unmowed grass. Grass! It looked as though I was standing on the edge of a park. And, hey, there was some clover! I was instantly beside the clover, squatting, fingering the heart-shaped leaves with their white markings. I didn't need my glasses to read into these familiar shapes and colors. I felt gladdened —much more at home. If there was a park and grass in this city, it couldn't be too strange.

Might there be a four-leaf clover? I began looking. I've always found it easy to find four-leaf clovers. As four-leaf clover folks know, it's possible to "sense" them before you see them. So, sensing one was close, I had to look, and...I woke up!

While I was happy to find myself in my own bed—not alone in some strange city—I was also, funny to say, slightly disappointed not to be hunting for this four-leaf clover! It wasn't the "luck" of the four-leaf clover I wanted, though that might have been helpful in the dream situation I'd landed in. What I wanted was the little "Got it!" satisfaction of sensing the presence of a four-leaf clover and connecting with it.

As I lay in bed mulling over the dream, it occurred to me how different my dependence on my eyes (and eyeglasses) is from the "sense" of the presence of a four-leaf clover. I'm not denying the role and import of the physical senses. Yet I have this other *sense*, a sense I may not be able to define very well, but one which I also can't deny. It was as though the dream was reminding me, no matter how confusing and scary the situation I may find myself in outwardly, there are within me subtle senses which, if I pay attention to them, can help to calm, steady, and reorient me.

I thought too how the absence of my glasses fed into my panic, while the realization I was on my own two feet stirred confidence. Then followed feelings of awe, wonder, and gratitude for the sky, sun, stars above and the earth below, which helped to anchor me not only in the strange world I'd found myself in, but in myself as well.

And that night I fell back asleep thinking: are we ever fully conscious of all the ties we have, both obvious and subtle, known and unknown, within the many worlds we inhabit and their possibilities? This is what Incarnational Spirituality is about: waking up to these connections.

First Language
Freya Secrest
June 2017

A friend and I were talking recently about the many ways we perceive and interpret the world through our subtle senses. She shared a conversation in which someone made the statement, "My first language is intuition." That statement got me thinking about what I would consider as my "first language". How do I first connect with and hear the world? How did it first speak in return? How might I widen my perception in order to better understand and communicate with others?

As I slow down and tune into my personal process of communication, it is clear to me that I perceive the world through patterns of movement. I notice the way a person holds their body, how upright they stand, where their shoulders fall. I gather impressions from their rhythm of walking. These impressions are my first forms of meaning-making and connection building. Next, I might listen to their tone of voice or the speed of their conversation. Only then do I register the words they are saying.

Following this track, I find that I need to widen my definition of languages beyond the verbal. When my children were small, I remember asking them to "use their words" rather than grabbing or crying to get something they wanted. It was an important step to help them understand their feelings and gain more direction and control of their energy. As I consider it now, I see that my instruction in itself recognizes that an exchange of information includes verbal, emotional, and energetic communication. Our familiarity with all three elements influences our ability to interpret and "language" our experience.

A language helps us to receive information, interpret it, and communicate to others. A language builds connection. Words can build those bridges and they are certainly the form most consciously used for exchange in our culture. But they are only one way to communicate an experience. Emotional and energetic languages also are tools of communication when we learn how to access them.

Once I was walking in the woods and I passed by a small grove of cedar trees. Focused on the path I was walking, I unexpectedly had the sensation of being called out to. "Hey! Over here!" It was as if I had walked by a group of people and had ignored them. When I looked around, I became aware that the trees were calling out to me. As I turned towards them, I felt a warm fellowship. It was a palpable feeling of walking through a field of communion.

But multi-sensory information is not new to the subtle realms of our world. While we humans have privileged spoken language and only recently have come to recognize auditory, visual, and kinesthetic senses as part of our communication platform, other realms communicate fluently through all these and a more formative language—the language of love and shared being. It is not specifically auditory, kinesthetic, or visual though it can use any and all of those forms. Love communicates through qualities such as respect, honor and joy, and the energy of our intention in action. It is with these languages that we build our fluency for communicating in Gaia's subtle ecology of life.

To widen into a deeper framework for communication, we need to be able to articulate our felt energies as well as connect feeling with our mental concepts and subtle experiences. Like light coming into a room from several windows, using multiple streams of information gives a wider perspective of what we are sensing. It is possible that when we are rooted more deeply into our natural form of connecting with the world that we will be better able to navigate other forms of expression and build bridges of understanding with each other.

There are so many languages I might like to learn. I have friends who speak Portuguese, French, science, and honeybee. Our world can speak wind and storm and drought and warm rain, but I think under it all our first language, love, shines light through all of our windows.

Finding Hearts
Susan Beal
November 2019

As the saying goes, "Seeing is believing," but it is equally true that "Believing is seeing." They are not opposites, and yet they're often perceived that way, just as a rational, scientific world view is often seen as the opposite of a spiritual, magical world view. So it's good to remember that we shape the world and the world shapes us—and there is magic in that.

My husband, David, and I just returned from a long camping trip, traveling cross country with our camper van from Vermont, through Michigan and the northern states to Washington, down the coast to California, cross the Mojave desert to Santa Fe, and then eastward toward home. We like to collect heart-shaped rocks when we travel, to bring home as a memento of the places we've been. We have a large collection of them on our mantlepiece, from many places around the US and the world. On our camping trip, we found heart-shaped rocks on the shores of the Great Lakes, on riverbanks in Montana, at ferry docks in Washington, ocean beaches and redwood forests in California, and even in a few parking lots and truck stops along the way.

It usually takes a bit of time to find a good heart-shaped rock. Sometimes there are very few candidates and the best we can do is find a rock with only the vaguest resemblance to a heart. But more often, we can find at least one rock with a definite, if slightly distorted, heart shape—good enough to bring home and add to our collection.

Finding something is as much about filtering out what you don't want as it is about finding what you do want. You have to set your intention and have a focus, a perceptual lens that filters what you're seeing in favor of what you're looking for. We all do this all the time, consciously and unconsciously, as a way of managing the continuous stream of information coming in from the worlds within and around us. Unfortunately, it's the same feature that sets us up for bias and prejudice and limits what we sense or comprehend. We lose the ability to see things we aren't looking for or don't believe in. And even if we do believe, the climate of skepticism that characterizes our world acts like smog in the atmosphere, clouding all but the most confident and acute perception.

One morning of our camping trip, we were staying at a campground in Big Sur, California. I ventured down to explore the bank of the Big Sur River, which ran through the campground, and sent out a little request to find a heart-shaped rock that might like to come home with us. It wasn't long before I found a nice one. I pocketed it, delighted with my find. Then I found another, and then several more.

I started getting quite selective, searching for the ever-more perfectly shaped heart rock. As I looked around, I began to see heart-shaped rocks everywhere, in every size, in every color and texture—elongated ones, squat wide ones, chunky and flattened ones, lumpy ones and smooth. They were grey, white, black and red, speckled, striped and solid. The more I looked, the more there were.

I think our brains are hardwired to feel good when we find things we're looking for, probably because our hunter gatherer ancestors relied on it to survive. Pleasure centers in the brain light up so we keep searching for roots and berries and rabbits. I felt the same urgent glee on the river bank each time I found another heart-shaped rock. I had started out hoping to find one, maybe two, but when more and more appeared, I felt compelled to keep gathering them. Each one I found led to another, like a trail of crumbs that might lead me to The Perfect Heart-Shaped Rock.

After a while, however, I began to feel odd, a bit disoriented, as if I had slipped into a reality where my intention was having an effect on the material world. It felt, suddenly, as if my desire to find a heart-shaped rock was magically affecting the rocks on the beach, as if little nature spirits—reading my desire—were quickly shaping rocks into hearts and setting them out for me to find.

It felt like manifesting on overdrive or like being in a semi-lucid dream. I once read about ways to test if you are dreaming or awake. One of them is to jump. If you stay aloft or float gently down, you are probably dreaming. If you don't, you're probably awake. I jumped on the beach and landed with the usual thump. But there were still heart-shaped rocks appearing everywhere, nestled among the non-heart-shaped rocks like a bumper crop of nuts. And the sense of magic persisted.

My heart opened, my perception widened, and everything intensified—the glitter of sun on the river water, the ratchety calls of jays and ravens in the redwoods, the scent of campfire ashes. I fell into a slight trance. I felt suffused with gratitude. Time dropped away.

But after a while my logical brain reasserted itself. Maybe, my inner skeptic rationalized, the endorphin buzz I got when I found a heart-shaped rock was prejudicing how I saw things. Maybe I was projecting heart shapes onto what were really just dented triangles and ovals, just to get that little rush.

But no. There really were a lot of rocks shaped like hearts.

Okay, my logical brain argued, there could be a geological or hydrological factor involved in the formation of rocks that looked kind of like hearts. Maybe this spot in Big Sur, on this particular riverbank, had just the right conditions.

It's possible there was some kind of geological explanation. It's possible my perception was biased. It's possible a bit of magic was involved. It may well have been a combination of influences. But finally, I realized what mattered was not the explanation—magical, perceptual, geological, or otherwise—for why there were so many heart-shaped rocks in one place. What mattered was that I found an abundance of what I was looking for and it made me happy.

I set aside a few of the best rocks to take home and made a mandala on the riverbank of the rest. I kept having to make it bigger as I kept finding more heart-shaped rocks. I have no idea if it's still there, or how many campers may have come upon it, or what they thought. But I like to think it made them happy, maybe even inspired them to look for more heart-shaped rocks to add to the mandala. And I imagine the energetic imprint of all of those heart shapes rippling outward, at least for a time, boosting the happiness quotient in that campground and even a bit beyond.

The most primal part of our nervous systems is designed to scan for threats, an instinctive bias that kicks into high gear whenever we're traumatized or just overly stressed. When it's activated, we interpret even the most benign things—a stick on the ground, a stranger's frown, an unusual sound—as dangerous. We live in challenging times and our limbic systems have a rough time of it. The news media is biased toward disaster and if the headlines are to be believed, there's little good in the world. It's the rare person whose nervous system is not generating anxiety, seeking something to worry about.

Imagine the effect this has, not only our own experience of the world, but on the planet itself: millions of human nervous systems primed to see danger everywhere, interpreting their surroundings as inhospitable, their fellow humans as untrustworthy, the earth as sick and dying.

Now imagine the effect of millions of people scanning for things that make them happy—heart-shaped rocks, or the kindness of strangers, or the verification of hope. We can try to find an explanation that pares wonder down into something mundane and reasonable.

Or we can see what happens when we start looking for hearts and finding them, everywhere.

Chapter 3: Into the Shadows

Me and My Shadow
Mary Reddy
March 2017

I once was wildly attracted to a man who was my teacher. Because I was afraid of my father, I resisted acting on the longing this man stirred in me. My heart had learned that harm would inevitably follow. Even more, he reminded me of everything I loved about my brothers. Lacking any sisters and with burdened parents, I had looked to my brothers for love, absorbing my family's distorted story about the masculine. I spent years running from men who carried the same qualities as my brothers, the intellectual drive and curiosity, a dominating male confidence covering a deep vulnerability. Because this teacher reminded me so much of my brothers, I loved him wildly from the first moment. And that terrified me. I flung myself into deep shadow work.

I had only recently emerged from a broken marriage. I was in the midst of painfully re-breaking myself in order to reset the bones of my heart and soul to heal properly. Fortunately, I was conscious enough of how much he churned up in me. I sensed this man was not what I thought him to be. He was a wonderful person, no doubt, but I was seeing in him those qualities that had lived in the heart of my family identity, all that I had known of love in my childhood.

Perhaps one clue to the disconnect between who he was and what I ascribed to him was that he gave me attention and treated me kindly—not something I experienced very often in my childhood. But I could not see who he was clearly enough, through the shimmer of what I projected upon him. Working with this awareness, I emerged on the other side better able to see others as they really are.

An early memory comes to mind where I struggled with my sense of self. My parents' friends had brought their toddler to a gathering—an adorable curly haired girl just a few years younger than I was. She became the center of attention and the adults exclaimed over her. I started following her around the room, mimicking her every move. This made her uncomfortable. She turned to look at me with fear in her eyes and she began to cry. The adults yelled at me to stop. I was astounded. Who was I to make a little girl afraid of me? Why had I behaved like that? Wasn't I a good little girl? I always tried to be good! What I did not realize at that age was how much I wanted the praise and attention that was being showered on the other little girl. My shadow self had sneaked out and taken over.

Once I met the shadow while reading the Bible. I became obsessed with Judas Iscariot, the man who betrayed Jesus to the Romans for thirty pieces of silver. I was in grade school then. I loved the rituals of the Catholic liturgical year. Holy Week was particularly intense. Praying at the stations of the cross, contemplating Christ's every encounter, each painful wound, was both oppressive and mesmerizing. That Good Friday ritual followed the previous evening's retelling of the Last Supper, when Jesus said that one of his disciples will betray him. He turns to Judas and tells him, "What you are about to do, do quickly."

I worried a great deal about Judas. Hadn't God placed on him the burden of being the betrayer? Surely, someone had to create the circumstances leading to Jesus's capture and ultimate sacrifice on the cross. God must have asked this of him and then forgiven him, I reasoned, otherwise it would be unfair. Maybe I worried that some part of Judas was in me. Unwittingly, I carried the shame that my father disavowed. That shame in me recognized the shame in Judas. I knew what it felt like to be the outsider, to be judged harshly, to be left on your own to figure out what little of value you could grab. I was hungry for love and convinced on a deep level that it was my fault that I went wanting. Now I wonder, was Judas the shadow side of Jesus? He was an indispensable part of the drama, yet he was the part that everyone wanted to disappear.

The shadow is our missing half—all those aspects of the self which we bury out of sight in order to win love or ensure safety. When we project onto another, we unconsciously surface a shadow element by assigning it to another. Such projection can be positive as well as negative. Perhaps we buried a vital talent of ours because we were scolded for appearing to be better than others. Then we lend that positive trait to another, elevating them to a pedestal that must inevitably topple. Whether positive or negative, projection generates discomfort all around.

In my hero's tale, as is true for anyone, I am at the center of events. I am the core actor, the Rosetta Stone, the sifter of meaning for everything that happens in and around me. In this central position, I project an image that fulfills what I believe about myself. I may shift emphasis, for example, pushing forward logical thinking and suppressing whimsy or intuition if the situation calls for it. But generally, this is the sphere of what I know and consciously acknowledge about who I am. I used to just barely tolerate this face I presented to the world. It was not the best of me. I believed that my better self lived in mystery, in my art, and in my dreams. But by just tolerating who I was in the world, was I not depriving myself of my own love, even as I'd felt deprived in childhood? What is the shadow of disliking who you are? I had always assumed it was an overweening egotism. Perhaps it's actually true compassion and love.

Studying the journey into fire, into the life path of the emerging soul, I began to soften into myself. Accepting both the rough and the polished sides of my personality led to a great curiosity and openness around who I am—beyond, behind, and within my public-facing self. I began to love myself, resting more firmly in my incarnate self, in this life of mine. And the openness and compassion I offer to myself travels more freely outward to others.

Now I watch for my shadow out of the corner of my eye. I open up to my possible selves. I posit the opposite of what I know I am feeling, to test the flavor, to see if I actually carry it as well. I imagine holding a brilliant prism up to the light. The facet facing me is my personality. Teasing out what's hidden in my shadow is like turning the prism this way and that. The quality of the light shifts. Each band of rainbow colors takes on more or less emphasis. Both white and multicolored, both whole and differentiated.

Reconciling India
Susan Beal
June 2018

My husband, David, and I went to India for two weeks in December. Siddhant, a beloved exchange student we hosted many years ago, was getting married. His family arranged for us to spend a week with them for the wedding festivities. We decided to spend a second week at a spiritual community planned around utopian ideals that we hoped would be restful after the wedding week.

There is little to rival the beauty and splendor of an Indian wedding. It was an overwhelmingly sensual experience—food rich with ghee and spices, henna paste painted in intricate designs onto our hands, trumpets and drums beating out wedding cadences, riotous dancing in the blazing sun, dazzlingly embellished clothing—everything swirling and teeming with colors, sounds, flavors and textures so unlike our quiet life in rural Vermont.

As Sid's "American parents," we were welcomed as honored guests and treated like family. We participated in pre-wedding rituals we barely understood, were fed more Gujarati wedding food than we could handle and were loaned traditional clothing so we were properly attired. Everyone wanted to meet us and tell us stories about Siddhant and his family or ask us how we liked India. Despite cultural differences between traditional Indian and American weddings, there were enough similarities to provide context and give us an emotional anchor. Through it all, we felt supported and protected by the warm hospitality of Siddhant's family. And had we returned home at the end of that week, our trip to India might simply have been a delightful, if at times overstimulating, experience.

But as soon as we left for the Chennai airport and boarded the plane for Pondicherry, we had no one to mediate or interpret the intensity of India for us. I hadn't realized how much the energy field of Siddhant's family had buffered us from the psychic and sensory extremes of India. The sheer sensory overload began to catch up to me as soon as we left, not only from the wedding week, but from the scenery that flashed by us in disturbing polarities: ancient temples, ornately carved; gaunt, hard-faced women cooking meals for their children on rubble-strewn sidewalks;

waves glittering on the Bay of Bengal; waiflike child beggars tapping on car windows; glossy cows strolling majestically through green fields; mounds of plastic trash tangled in the roots of banyan trees.

I suspect many of the readers of this blog, like me, are very sensitive to energies and environmental influences. I'm particularly sensitive to sound. I'm used to mostly natural sounds in Vermont—wind, birds, the sound of the brook, an occasional passing car. India was teeming with people, colors, noises, and smells unlike anything at home. The racket in India exacerbated the difficulty of taking in so many unfamiliar sights. The cacophony of two-stroke rickshaw engines, diesel engines, blaring horns, barking dogs, rattling air conditioners, cement drills, and jack hammers made it hard to find my own center.

Despite my sensitivity, David and I are easy-going people. Normally we'd have taken such things in stride as an expected part of adventure in a new place. But we also knew we'd need down time to maintain our equilibrium. We thought we'd arranged for just that—a quiet, contemplative week to digest the wedding experience. Instead, the community we'd hoped would be peaceful and welcoming was opaque and almost impenetrable to casual visitors. We'd envisioned a serene setting, a meditative oasis, but the same scenes of deprivation and suffering were everywhere on the outskirts. Our guest house room, though clean, was stark and ill-lit, and filled with curry fumes from the kitchen exhaust fan below our glassless window. Hot water and electricity were intermittent. To top it off, we'd both picked up parasitic infections in the first week – the infamous Delhi belly. It seemed fitting that my digestive system was roiling along with my emotions.

The morning after we arrived at the community, we came upon a tiny puppy lying, unmoving, in the heat of the sun by the side of the road. The owner of the café nearby said the puppy had been hit by a motor bike. He seemed unconcerned and his apathy was understandable. Why worry about one little dog in the midst of so much other human and animal suffering? The wall my heart had built to cope with the grief and intensity of India started to crack. I wanted to help the puppy. I wanted to walk away and not face the tide of utter helplessness I'd felt since we'd arrived. I didn't want to drown in that tide I'd held at bay, and I struggled as I stood there, between opening my heart or closing it, trying to help or turning away. I struggled with my American assumptions in the midst of Indian realities. Suddenly it felt like a test, my heart being weighed on a scale.

Hesitantly, I asked the café owner for a bowl of water and a towel. I washed the puppy's wounds, nestled her in the towel, and blessed her. I resolved to find out if there was an animal shelter or at least a concerned person who might help. I couldn't do anything for the begging children, or the women raising families on landfills, or the skeletal cows eating trash, but I could do something for this puppy. I clung to her welfare in the midst of my overwhelm as a tiny act of love I could take to buoy my drowning heart.

I teach a form of meditation called Yoga Nidra, which means yogic sleep. It's deeply restful and restorative, but one of the most powerful practices within it is called playing with opposites. First you focus awareness on, say, an emotion like fear, noticing how it feels in the body. Then you focus on the opposite emotion—perhaps safety. Then you move back and forth, noticing differences in how the body responds. And then you hold both opposites in awareness simultaneously— hard to do intellectually, but revelatory when you surrender to it as a felt sense in the body.

We tend to think of opposites as, well, opposite; but in practicing yoga nidra, I've discovered that sometimes they're the same energy in the body, just interpreted differently by the mind or psyche. For instance, joy and grief feel strangely similar—a strong sensation of energy in the heart—although, given my different associations with them, they moved differently in my body. Grief feels stuck and lumpy; joy shines and flows. Yet when merged, they melt into each other and become a radiance in my heart center.

No matter how much we might try, we can't escape our cultural and individual biases and the way they influence our perception. In these times of increasing sensitivity to the flashpoints of prejudice and privilege, all I can claim about my experience of India is that it was mine, and it was up to me to integrate its extremes within the context of my own life. One day, while leaving the elegant courtyard of our inn, I almost stumbled on an old man lying in a heap of rags on the sidewalk. I looked at him and then around the street. People—locals and white tourists alike—were streaming past. I steeled myself and walked past, but my heart tore apart. It took the little puppy to help me find a way to back to my center. Tending to her helped me begin to reconcile the opposites of India in my heart. All the love and kindness I'd experienced during the wedding, all the horror and helplessness I'd felt in the face of so much deprivation and suffering, narrowed down to a single point when I decided to try to help that little puppy.

She made a seemingly miraculous recovery by the next morning. She was up and about and wagged her tail when she saw me. Even the café owner seemed surprised and happy by such a turnaround. But alas, we didn't save that puppy. We had gotten the name of a member of the Auroville community who worked at the animal sanctuary and promised to search for her. He never found her, although he found several others while searching and brought them to the safety of the sanctuary.

Our bodies can make sense of what to our minds may seem like irreconcilable differences. But because our intellects often resist what our bodies understand, the body often reconciles such extremes through illness or injury. I was nauseous and utterly without appetite for over two months after returning from India. I lost 15 pounds and felt anxious and haunted. I cocooned in my safe, quiet bedroom for days on end, grateful for silence and stillness in which to slowly decompress and integrate. The whole trip to India—the joy, the pathos, the beauty, the horror—seemed to pivot on the moment I decided to help that puppy. All I could do was surrender to my body's slow and steady healing and wait for my appetite and energy to return.

What I've learned from the practice of playing with opposites in yoga nidra is that wholeness springs, in part, from the willingness to embrace it. Wholeness is implicate and ever present, waiting for us to recognize it, but our resistance to bridging differences and our love of neat categories can make us blind to it. It's a common belief that beauty and joy are fragile, and even obscene in the face of suffering and degradation. We in the West seem to need dichotomies to make sense of the world. Our legal system is built on duality, as are our political and religious systems that define right and wrong for us. But the funny thing is, when you hold space for seeming opposites, when you really *feel* them in the body and the heart, the mind quiets down and paradoxes collapse. It's not unlike eating food, in which something that is entirely separate from us, through digestion, becomes part of us.

One morning in India, while stopped in traffic in our taxi, I saw a toddler in the meridian, tied by her ankle with a strip of plastic to a shrub. Trucks, cars and auto-rickshaws whizzed past her on all sides while she poured water from a plastic bottle into the dirt and patted the mud onto her bare legs. She looked happy, utterly absorbed in play. A woman I assumed was her mother was knocking on car windows ahead of us. Just beyond the woman, a young boy and girl dressed in tatters were trying to cross the busy highway. Arms linked, they skipped and danced between cars, advancing and retreating across lane after lane of chaotic traffic. They were laughing as if it was the best fun in the world to make it safely to the other side.

I cannot know what lies ahead for that mother and her children. It's difficult not to judge their lives from the standpoint of my own and I feel many varieties of guilt and confusion. But the obvious joy of those children is what stays with me the most. It is there, in that innocent union of joy and suffering, where wholeness lies, and our divided hearts heal.

What is the Role of Conscious Suffering?
Drena Griffe
November 2020

Recently the Lorian Association received the following question:

"I'm a person who has, for years now, been disillusioned by the new age focus of hope, light, butterflies, and 'if you tune into energies high enough and correctly, all will be well'. Life on this planet also includes pain. Life here is not life without suffering. These are realities. This duality is real.

My question: Is there a place for Conscious Suffering as a subtly chosen path? Or is this a 'compromise path' for those who 'faltered' along the way, a path for those of us who are less evolved?"

I too have witnessed the pressure in spiritual communities to conform to positions that exclude suffering, though I think this is far from being a "new age focus". From the moment human beings first invented the idea called belief, we also created a structure around it that associated misfortune with punishment.

It can be equally problematic, though, to attach oneself to conscious suffering. Many of us are spiritually sophisticated enough to recognize the importance of paradox, yet often the only ways we can think to create balance is to move to the side of the boat where fewer people sit. (I'm guilty of this!) We position ourselves in an either/or state, and cling to an idea of transcendence as an elevation above conflict.

Real transcendence is the ability to focus on the internal movement of spirit regardless of where we're sitting. A spiritual practice focused on either love and light, or suffering and pain, strikes me as our personalities clinging to stories about life, instead of accepting certain complexities that are simply part of the cost of admission.

I personally feel the beauty of Incarnational Spirituality lies in its simplicity. We are here—that means we belong. God exists anywhere we are. For me right now, God exists as a middle aged, brown-skinned cis heterosexual woman. This body and life is not just a suit that I must transcend in order to have a spiritual experience. It's an integral part of that experience. I have experienced racism, cruelty, sickness. I have been physically and emotionally abused. I have suffered health challenges.

At a glance, society would see me as marginalized in multiple ways. At times I have seen myself as a victim. Other times a survivor. All of these versions hold some truth.

Yet I also recognize that when I said yes to this strange and surreal adventure, God chose to express itself through me in this particular form and shape. And I came here to experience something, to achieve something, to be something here in an incarnated form that really isn't possible without a body, mind, spirit and complex set of emotions. There are things we all came to do that really aren't possible anywhere except on earth in skin suits of humanity.

Having said that, I don't wish to ignore conscious suffering completely. Life on earth does seem to require some suffering. Why? Spiritual teacher Reverend Cynthia Bourgealt once illustrated the reasons as part of a lecture series I listened to a handful of years ago. Here is a summary of what I learned:

God, the One, the Almighty, was undivided. An infinite artist and creator always seeks to unlock their own potential, so God divided itself into an infinite number of expressions of self. In one incarnation, God chose to be, say, a gay priest struggling to come to terms with the church's teachings and their inner experience. In another incarnation, God chose to be that priest's father torn between what they had been taught of right and wrong and love for their child. Both are expressions of the same God.

How can we not have suffering on Earth with so many different incarnate expressions of Oneness running around loose? God's experience of Themself generates conflict. Why? It's because God wants to expand beyond God's own limitations. Expansion requires tension.

I know this view may be difficult to accept. We don't easily identify as divine expressions any people or forces whose actions create opposition to our values. Yet every person that lives and has ever lived has a purpose in being here. Apart from the inherent challenge in this statement is the fact that resistance to the Sacredness within others often masks a resistance to the Sacredness within ourselves.

The Compromise Path

I find it interesting how our human minds got it twisted that an absence of conflict equates with a more spiritually evolved person. I'd say the opposite is true. The truly evolved people are the heavy lifters. A sweeping glance at modern history immediately produces a few outstanding characters: Victor Frankl, Etty Hillesum, John Lewis. In moments when I feel like I've had all that I can take of challenging conditions on planet Earth, I look to *Man's Search for Meaning* by Victor Frankl (Beacon Press, 1962) and *An Interrupted Life* by Etty Hillesum (Pantheon Books, 1983). I don't know how anyone could walk away from the Holocaust with their spirit intact, but Victor Frankl did. Etty Hillesum died at Auschwitz in 1943, and her journal stands as a testament to the resiliency of the human mind, body and spirit to transcend suffering by wholly embracing the state of one's life exactly as it is. My father recently shared with me a similar degree of respect for civil rights leader and US senator John Lewis: *I don't know how that man survived what he did and still loved people.*

It seems to me that the lightweights are those who surround themselves with "love and light", and retreat from any experience which contradicts their ideas of spiritual abundance. *If God loves me, then he will bless me with happiness, comfort and ease.* There's nothing wrong with desiring a life free of pain; however, true spiritual abundance is the ability to connect with the God within oneself, no matter one's external circumstances. It's finding the Sacred inside the Fire.

On September 30, 1942, just over a year before she was slaughtered in a Nazi concentration camp, Etty Hillesum wrote a personal testament in the midst of collective despair:

"… if you destroy the ideas behind which life lies imprisoned as behind bars … then you will also have the strength to bear real suffering, your own and the world's."

No matter who we are, where we are, and the darkness of the times in which we live, there is a path of light. Truly, the only compromise that I can see lies in the denial of even the tiniest aspect of our human experiences, no matter how overwhelming it may seem in moments of vulnerability. I don't think we need to consciously seek out suffering as a life choice. Instead, we should open heartedly accept the unfolding of our lives in fullness. After all, they, with their particular difficulties and graces, are the places where the Gods within us seek to embrace the world.

Dancing with the Shadow
Julia Spangler
March 2019

As a parent, I recall the very special experience of watching my children learn about their world, often seeing myself in them, remembering how full of wonder the world really is. I saw a video the other day of a toddler seeing her shadow on the ground for the first time and running screaming away from this dark thing that kept following her. I laughed to see it, of course, because it is funny from the perspective of people who know what this dark thing is. But from this child's perspective, it was terrifying. This is the way it is with the unknown and is why we spend so much time and effort avoiding it.

The shadow has become a powerful meme in our modern culture. I think there are few, at least in the western world, who are not familiar with the idea of the shadow as a representation of the unconscious parts of our personality. Carl Jung is probably best known for his recognition of the shadow archetype as the representation of our dark side—all that we refuse to look at in ourselves. But it has been well represented in our culture through the arts—visual, theatrical and literary—throughout history.

The Star Wars story may be the best known modern exploration of the shadow, with the innocent hero, Luke Skywalker, confronting his darker nature (represented by his father, Darth Vader) in order to win freedom. By understanding and accepting his dark side, he also redeems that of his father, freeing Darth Vader from the grip of his own shadow self.

But my favorite shadow story is one by Ursula LeGuin, *The Wizard of Earthsea* (Parnassus Press, Berkeley, 1968). This wizard starts the story as a young man, Ged, who is born with a talent for magic, which earns him a place in the prestigious school for wizards on the famous Isle of Roke. (This school predated Hogwarts by some decades, I must say.) Now, Ged is young and inexperienced in the world, coming from a small village in the mountains. He knows little of the world, and even less about himself. Thus, when the unconscious elements of his personality rise up, he has little defense. He encounters another student at the school who, while being older and of a higher birth, has less talent. Both boys find themselves at the mercy of the little shadows we call jealousy and pride, of course denying both. These attributes are shoved into the background of their consciousness because they are threatening!

One sorry night, Ged is challenged by his rival to a magical competition during which Ged, trying to prove how powerful he is, opens a door into the shadow realms and unleashes a dark power into the world. Ged is haunted by this shadow, running from it, fearing it, is disempowered by it, and finally realizes that he cannot leave it loose in the world. He must hunt it down. Once he turns to hunt it, this fearsome thing runs! Until then Ged has been running from it in terror, and it has gained power over him. Suddenly when he faces it, it runs! Ged knows he must name this shadow in order to command it back into its place. The story takes him through many adventures as he hunts for the name of this thing. But in the end, upon catching up to the shadow being, Ged finally knows its name and names it—"Ged". The two step into each other and become one. Ged is whole and free.

I have used this story in classes, since it is a wonderful allegory for dealing with our own inner shadows. That which we fear will have power over us and we will spend much energy defending ourselves from it. What we deny will sneak up on us and take us by surprise. What we can become conscious of, what we can name, becomes part of our wholeness, part of our power.

A friend of mine told me of a dream she had a while ago which shows another way of approaching the shadow. She was being chased by a giant spider, running for her life. The spider was gaining on her and her terror drove her faster. Finally, recognizing that it was going to catch her, and she would die, she turned to face it. As she did, and started walking toward it, the spider grew smaller and smaller until she reached down and picked it up. Here was something that was actually a beautiful and fascinating creature. Another powerful image for handling these shadow parts of ourselves. Stop running, turn and truly look at it. What gift is there?

As adults, we carry much from our past that is held as shadow. We have learned to be wary, to self-censor, and to fear. These are not attributes which encourage our light to shine. To be willing to take risks and surrender to the recognition that we are not perfect, to allow ourselves to see the flawed parts and name them, is to be freed from the past and to become new.

It is that unencumbered newness which we so enjoy seeing in children. When my own child, Aidan, was a toddler, I had the pleasure of being present when she first saw her shadow. We were outside in the sun, and Aidan saw it on the garage door. She stopped in surprise, staring at this dark shape. She moved, it moved. She stopped, it stopped. She lifted her arms and the arms of the shadow rose too. She turned around and looked back, watching the shadow intently. She jumped and watched its feet lift off the ground. Then Aidan started to dance with it. I thought, "What a wonderful model for engaging with the shadow!"

Seeing in the Dark
Susan Beal
April 2017

I started wearing glasses when I was in fourth grade. At first I was excited—they were something new, and it was fun to see so clearly! But after a while I started to resent how they split the world into things I could see well within a little oval frame, and things outside the oval that were blurry. I learned to feel anxious without glasses, dependent on them to make the outer world clear to me.

In my teens, I became interested in vegetarianism, herbology, and various alternative approaches to health, and wondered why eyesight seemed like the only part of our well-being that we couldn't heal. I took a number of natural vision improvement programs and read various books about it, but I wasn't able to cure my myopia. In fact, my prescription grew stronger through the years. Even so, I kept thinking there must be a link between the eyes and our overall well-being, a link that might explain why such a big percentage of modern humanity needs corrective lenses.

Not long ago, I went to a weekend course on natural vision improvement, this one based not on nutrition and eye exercises, but on the idea that our eyesight is a direct result of how we think about ourselves and the world as well as what we believe about reality.

The instructor told us that the anatomy of the human eye tells an interesting story about perception and consciousness. Only about 5 percent of the photoreceptor cells on our retinas—the cones—are devoted to the acuity, color, and detail that characterize daylight vision. The other 95 percent—the rods—are devoted to night and peripheral vision, to shadows and movement, and they are nearly 1,000 times more sensitive than our cones. Our rods, he said, are not only a major part of whole vision, but intimately tied to our subconscious brain activity and the parts of our psyche involved with dreaming, imagination, and non-ordinary reality. In other words, our eyes are superbly designed to see in the dark, both literally and metaphorically, yet we rarely use them that way.

The instructor said one of the most healing things we can do for our vision and our psyches is to spend at least half an hour every day using our eyes in the dark. It takes at least half an hour of darkness before our eyes are dark-adapted and the rods come fully online, so to speak. Meditating or lying in bed with eyes shut doesn't count. "By cultivating night vision, we nourish our retinas," he said, "and we also nourish the part of our mind that knows and perceives things beyond the conscious, well-lit, everyday world."

Which to me begs the question: what happens when we routinely rely on little more than 5 percent of our visual capacity? When we don't take the time to see in the dark, might all kinds of wonders and mysteries we might otherwise perceive become nothing but vague shadows, things to be feared, ignored, or forgotten? For the first time in history, more than half the world's population is urban. It's significant for many reasons, not the least of which, to my mind, is that for the first time in the history of the world, most of humanity never experiences true darkness or a night sky black enough to see stars. Even for those of us who live in the country, it's rare to spend 30 minutes or more awake in the darkness. Most of us keep the lights on until we lie down to go to sleep, and even then many folks have some kind of light in the room, intentionally or not. Given the link between night vision and the subconscious, is it any wonder that the world of dreams, of subtle perceptions, of imagination and realities beyond the physical realm, are dismissed as unreal? And is it any surprise that anxiety, the harbinger of information from the subconscious, is pandemic?

There's a traditional Scottish poem that goes: "From Ghoulies and Ghosties and long leggedy Beasties and Things that go bump in the Night, May the Good Lord deliver us." Before electricity, we spent half our lives in darkness. Whether the light and darkness was equally divided each day, as near the equator, or divided up by the season, as toward the poles, we spent many hours awake and seeing in the dark. Perhaps it explains why we also had more tacit acceptance of— as well as more overt fear of—the shadow realms. We couldn't simply shut out the specters or scatter our demons by turning on a light. We couldn't medicate our fear or dismiss as superstition anything that couldn't be explained by scientific means.

Similar to the percentage of cones to rods, it's often said that only about 5 percent of the activity of our brains is conscious, with the other 95 percent being unconscious. It's also supposed that the percentage of ordinary matter in the universe is about 4 percent. The rest is dark matter and dark energy. To me, there is an interesting pattern here. The conscious mind likes things neat and tidy, black and white, rational and physical. But it turns out those things are only a tiny percentage of what's out there to know and perceive.

In addition to the lining of rods and cones on the retina, there is an area called the fovea, where the optic nerve connects and there are no rods or cones. It leaves a blind spot in the very center of our vision. In daylight, it's hardly noticeable. But at night, if you try to look directly at a star, it will disappear, thanks to the blind spot. As with stars at night, many things are difficult if not impossible to see by looking directly at them. Instead, we need to open our vision wide and pay attention to the edges and peripheries, the liminal zones. The vision instructor taught us to stop trying to see accurately or clearly, and instead to try to see panoramically, with a wide perspective instead of a narrow focus. This approach, he assured us, would allow us to see more of what was really out there. He also said to let the light and darkness come into our eyes as if we were letting the world in, rather than staring at the world like a movie screen that is either in focus or not.

And good vision is not just about accuracy, color, and clarity. There are ambiguities, fuzzy places, shadows, and movements we can't always clearly define. There is a parallel between approaching this liminal, shadowy boundary of daytime and nighttime perception, and the classic boundary between the everyday, human world and the mutable, shadowy realms of faeries and spirits and the things we have forgotten how to see or might rather not know. It's reminiscent of dream recall, that moment between dreaming and wakefulness when the memory of a dream can seem as intangible and fragile as a wisp of mist in bright, hot sunlight. Even the memory of inner journeys and meditations can be hard to bring back into normal, daily consciousness, unless written down or recited while one is still between states of mind.

As physical beings, we are grounded in a world of duality, of matter and spirit, of shadow and light, of conscious and unconscious. We are the bridges between realms, and we can learn to see beyond that duality, toward the wholeness of the world within and outside us.

It begins by learning to see in the dark.

The Gift of Darkness
Mary Reddy
February 2018

"Darkness rises and Light to meet it," says Snoke, the Supreme Leader and super villain in *The Last Jedi*. This Star Wars tale and a thousand other legends are steeped in the eternal battle between good and evil. And the ultimate goal is eradication of evil, right? Oh boy, do we human beings struggle with that one. We worry, "but will we see that in our lifetimes? Or can evil actually prevail?" We must stay in the Light, we think, but what good does it do if we armor ourselves in it and depart from the world? Throughout the ages, countless folk tales and magical legends have obliquely touched on this difficult-to-describe conundrum of life on earth.

I've been considering the ways the Star Wars movies have satisfied (or failed) my craving for a good magical story. One thing I love, that repeatedly happens, is that the good guy goes to meet the bad guy. He goes into the very bowels of hell, into the Death Star, to stand face-to-face with evil. In other stories, say, a classic Western shoot-em-up, the hero goes to meet the villain in order to stop him and destroy him. But a different ethic comes into play in the Star Wars stories. Though stopping the bad guy is desirable, going to meet him is first and foremost a crucial step along the way of the hero becoming fully himself. Standing in the power of the Force, the good guy must confront and acknowledge how much he has in common with the evil one. Though fearful of what will ensue, the good guy musters his courage to go and face himself.

The Last Jedi goes even further. No longer requiring exclusively male pronouns (hurray!) to describe the hero's tale—the story pluralizes into a number of tales of diverse heroes. As I watched, I followed two new and different threads with growing fascination: the overturning of beloved icons and the waves of ambiguity washing over the dichotomy of good and evil.

That we live in time and experience change over time almost ensures that inevitably some beloved person, truth, manner of expression, cultural practice, or favorite way of seeing ourselves must pass away. What feels different about this time on earth is a growing sense of urgency around that necessity. We almost need to take apart and recreate what we love best (democracy, community, our place in nature) in order to avoid losing it (and ourselves) entirely.

We all instinctively understand the hero's journey. What's more difficult is how to see the path in the midst of the storm or fog of daily life. I was privileged to experience a complete breakdown early in my life. It was hard to go through, it was hard on my family, and at times it was hard to see a light at the end of the tunnel. But having emerged from it more whole, more balanced, I have a deep appreciation of the prize at the end of a descent into the shadows and a climb back up. Increased appreciation of all the elements that came together to form my life, deep gratitude for the love and assistance of the ones who stood by me as I fell apart. And even now, I am more likely to love and appreciate people who appear to be acting from a place of darkness.

My life is no longer about a dramatic descent and upward climb and it's trickier to see the path toward dramatic growth. In the new wholeness and balance that I gained, I find my growth pushing me toward more engagement with others, with community wherever I find it. I see so many of us (and our communities) living with uncertainty. We watch as the world wildly careens from one threat to another. One understandable response is to hold fast to old icons.

How do we entertain uncertainty around the once unquestioned duality of the moral universe? How do we pause before rushing to judgment? Polarization, duality, either/or—they overwhelmingly claim our public discourse and infect our ability to imagine solutions. What once worked as a dialectic (thesis, antithesis, synthesis) never proceeds to the synthesis. Maybe we need more than just two sides?

What if I were to go into the bowels of the earth to find myself by confronting the dark? Maybe my shadow is not so extremely dark, what if I am so many shades of grey? Instead of struggling to surface The Shadow, what if I discover a collective of lights and shadows that spin kaleidoscopically into consciousness and out. What if our imagined victory over the present crises cannot take shape until we crush the iconic opposition of two sides—why only two?

Suppose we start with a clean sheet and the first thing we write on it is love. Inhabiting a cellular, systems-drawn, neuron-firing, sometimes wave/sometimes particle-based, complex Gaian being such as ours, how many sides will love call forth?

Chapter 4: Into the Collective

And There Was Light
Claire Blatchford
December 2016

Shortly after the 2016 presidential election I felt the need to reconnect with someone I admire, someone whose way of being in the world has always been an inspiration to me. I've never met this man in person—only through his writings—yet regard him as a close friend.

Jacques Lusseyran may already be familiar to some of you. He is best known for his book *And There Was Light* (Morning Light Press, November 2000). He was born in Paris in 1924 and became totally blind from an accident when only eight years old. Yet he discovered early on as a child that, although he couldn't see in the usual way with his physical eyes, he could still see. And this "seeing" could grow, expand, and move in many different directions.

In his memoir, Jacques describes the beginning of this discovery as "looking from an inner place to one further within." He became aware of a radiance he said could have been outside him or within him, a light which brought relief, happiness, confidence and gratitude. As he wrote, "I found light and joy ... and...from that time (they) have never been separated in my experience. I saw light and went on seeing it though I was blind." (p. 16-17)

This may sound rather poetical to you—Jacques' writing is full of poetry—but for me, when I was 28 and first read of his different way of "seeing", his words were more than merely lyrical, they rang true. I, myself, am not blind but am profoundly deaf. Like Jacques I lost my hearing suddenly at a young age and began my journey into the discovery that there are many ways of hearing even if one's physical ears are damaged. The larger discovery though was that I, too, found confidence and gratitude in the "radiance" Jacques describes. And I, too, was unable to name this radiance as he did, till much later in my life. We can know and yet not know something. It's as though this light waits within us and, when I first read his book, my immediate response was, "Yes, I am pretty sure I know what he's talking about!" This is why I need now and then to return to his words, and the way he lived out his understanding of and connection with this light because I believe it can be found within each and all of us, especially when the darkness feels pronounced. As it does now in these confusing times.

In his book Jacques describes being able to "see" physical objects by way of the inner light. Because of it he was able to find his way not only around his home and the neighborhood he lived in, but when walking in the mountains as well. The light stimulated other forms of seeing within him. For example, in his home or neighborhood, the felt sense of familiar objects around him, their placement, the spaces between them and their light—for all that is incarnated has light—enabled him to "see" and thus to move with confidence. When in the mountains, an even deeper seeing was awakened, in such a way that Jacques could instinctively see the rise and fall of the land.

It took Jacques a long time to begin to find the right words to describe how he was able to "*see*" in this way. As he did so, two other things impressed themselves on his inner sense of vision. The first was a wonderful sense of the completeness, the oneness, of the world and the second was that the world comes to meet and greet one to the extent one steps forward to meet and greet it. Jacques experienced this in a poignant way through his hands when discovering as a child how everything he lifted or merely touched—be it a stone, apple, table, even the walls of the house his family lived in—responded, by way of a responding pressure.

Especially helpful to me when I was younger was Jacques' discovery that, if he was angry or fearful—in short, was not attuned to the light—he had great difficulty, stumbled, banged into things, was unable to find his way. This, in turn, made clear to me how I can become altogether deaf when I'm out of sorts, lacking in gratitude, oblivious to the radiance in the world and myself.

When Jacques was fifteen, Paris was invaded and the German occupation began. A year later, with a few close friends, he formed and headed an underground resistance movement of six hundred youths. Because of what his comrades called his "sense of human beings," Jacques was chosen to interview all recruits. He could "see" into men, could see the light or the dark of the thoughts they held in their hearts. Being able to use this seeing for the good of his country guided him day by day.

From there, Jacques' story took him into Buchenwald: the one man he was uncertain about was recruited and later betrayed Jacques and his comrades to the Nazis. That he came out alive, though mere skin and bones, and went on to become a husband, father, university professor, and writer was a testament to the Light within.

***

I hope at this point that I don't sound as though I'm just writing a review of a book which is both luminous and incredibly suspenseful. What became clear to me as I tracked down my heavily underlined copy is how very important the admiration connection is right now. It's said we become what we admire. In this time of ugly words, thoughts, and deeds I feel the need like a hunger: to draw close to the enlightened words, thoughts, and deeds of those I admire—here and on the other side too.

Jacques' discoveries as a blind man not only helped me make sense of my discoveries as a deaf woman, helping me to connect with the essential wholeness that is within every one of us (even if physically different or chronically ill), they showed how we can be blind and deaf in more ways than the physical. The conditions we are in can blind and deafen us to the light within and without. Jacques' message is more relevant now than ever: There *is* Light!

Movement of the Heart
Drena Griffith
July 2016

A painting of a white Jesus, blonde, blue-eyed, greeted us each afternoon as we walked into religion class my sophomore year of high school. On the same wall hung a black Jesus with dark skin and curly hair. These two images watched us quietly, day after day for months, until one of my classmates finally asked the question unspoken but clearly often wondered about: "Why is there a picture of a white Jesus and a black Jesus on the wall?"

In response, our religion teacher explained that the Jewish Jesus Christ, from the Middle East with olive colored skin and dark, wavy hair, really did not look like either representation. But what did we think?

Well, of course Christ had to be more white, several of my classmates exclaimed, because white represented everything important and good in our country and world, right? Of course Christ couldn't really be black because black people were inferior; hadn't history proven that time and again? What began as a discussion about wall hangings slowly turned bitter and aggressive as the rising tide of resentments over affirmative action, the Confederate flag, and other lingering issues of our parents' (and grandparents') days projected conflicting attitudes upon those images.

I was one of two non-white students sitting in the classroom the day the question was asked. At the time I felt deeply defensive, shamed and wounded by the words of my classmates, some of them my friends.

As for me, I really couldn't relate to either white or black Jesus. Neither image reflected my reality. It seemed to me that my classmates needed Jesus to be white because they were white. And they needed Jesus to not be black because of what they had been taught to believe about blackness. But hadn't I grown up on those same depictions, except within me whiteness also seemed remote and beyond my reach, and blackness as something to despise? Wasn't Jesus Christ—as the Bible stories portrayed him at least—selfless, conscientious and, above all else, inclusive?

Neither of those images told me a thing about the real Christ; though silent as they were, they seemed to reveal much of what we believed about each other.

Over twenty-six years later, I'm reminded of those silent, watchful paintings and that blistering conversation as I listen to the cultural and racial rhetoric of this season: *Black Lives Matter, All Lives Matter*. The two movements slam against each other, unyielding, the existence of one seemingly negating the stance of the other. Last week was particularly brutal and troubling. But when I hold the fresh wave of pain flowing across the nation from communities in Falcon Heights, Baton Rouge, and Dallas, I don't see white blood and black blood. I don't see an "us" versus "them". What I do sense is a commingled wave of fear, misunderstanding, and hatred that I know firsthand can sweep across and drag all colors and races, cultures and creeds, movements and good intentions down to the depths.

As someone who has actively contemplated and sought to reconcile racial discord since long before that fateful high school class discussion, the one—and perhaps only—thing I've come to understand is the complexity of the issues involved.

It seems to me that if we stop to think about it, of course it's true that "Black Lives Matter". And yes, it's equally true that "All Lives Matter". Standing alone, each is an expression of a very real incarnate need to be recognized and understood. The trouble is, these movements don't stand alone. The framework of each depends upon a particular discourse with the other; and often it seems what some people react against is what they think the other means by what it says.

Just like with the two images of Jesus on the wall, the issues ultimately had nothing at all to do with those images themselves, but what we as a class projected onto them. (Of course, that didn't make the resulting tension any less real. In fact, I think it made things worse. It's nearly impossible to find resolution when the issues themselves cast shadows.)

But my guiding principle in response to all social and political challenges is this: it doesn't matter what we profess to believe if our actions, even our anger at injustice, exclude us from those around us. Our neighbors. Our friends. Our enemies. *Them*, whoever that happens to be. In some ways, it doesn't matter how we wound up together in this place, because together we are. All of our fates intertwine. So either we all get home together, or no one does. In the end, beliefs should serve people, rather than the other way around.

But more and more I've come to see belief, even beliefs about race, as less a static basis of identity and more of a spectrum, a range diverse and multifaceted as our own distinct hues, features and cultural differences. I've also witnessed the existence of something opposite—vectors of unintegrated subtle energy that David Spangler refers to as "hungry Ghosts." I call them colorless holes. These energetic voids feed from our disconnection. They feed on the words that people don't feel comfortable sharing for fear of censure and trial by public opinion. They feed on the fears that people suppress. And they expand and engulf entire sections of our world when people react and become filled, even with justifiable wrath and rage in response to discrimination.

Truly, it's hatred, rather than love, that knows no color. Its counterforce, love, by its very nature embraces all, including and especially that which challenges it. That makes love itself a multifaceted, multicolored experience.

Of course, none of this is an answer to the racial challenges facing the United States (and our world.) There aren't easy answers. Quite frankly there may not be answers at all. I know we must stand against injustice. I know we must not yield to rage in our quest for understanding. But this past week especially there seemed to be such a narrow space in between those two points that it's been all I personally could do to stand still, say a firm clear no the energies of that devouring, colorless void and, as quietly as possible, attune my heart to love that knows a world where all races existing in harmony is possible.

It has to live in me, and be nourished by the soil of my efforts and responses first and foremost. So taking a quiet hour, after a week of violence and anger, I look towards the movement stirring within my own heart, and I ask myself: *How do I find love in this hour, in this place, where I am? How do I love and honor all victims of racial violence so that their sacrifices aren't in vain? How do I love white police officers using excessive force against unarmed and innocent people? How do I love black men shooting white officers in retaliation? How do I love my friends, black, white, and all shades in between, struggling in sometimes awkward, conflicting ways to make sense of these trials? How do I love myself, love the limitations and resistances I sometimes encounter right here at home in this heart—the part of me that wants to give in and give up?*

This is my humble offering to this hour of painful struggle. Today I hold my silent vigil and tomorrow I will seek out ways to act upon it. I will bless every cop I see. I will honor every one of my friends brave enough to speak out openly and honestly. I will partner with them to paint a new portrait of our world. I will risk openness and discomfort and share my own deeper feelings. Day by day, hour by hour, moment by moment—I will not give into fear.

***

That afternoon in religion class as white Jesus and black Jesus looked on us with solemnity and sadness in their eyes, I could not easily see something that seems obvious to me now: our teacher never asked us to choose one painting over the other. We took on that task ourselves. Yet over these long years, in the times when I've seen the essence of Christ truly reflected in the world around me, it has never seemed more clear how similar we all are beneath the boundary we call skin. In fact, I cannot help being reminded of the immortal words of poet Maya Angelou in her poem "Human Family":

"…we are more alike, my friends, than we are unalike." (Random House, 1990)

Strange Attractors
Susan Beal
August 2017

I have had a meditation and spiritual practice for almost 40 years. Mostly it's been a private thing, central to my sense of self and informing my activities in the outer world, but never overt. In many ways, my experiences of the "inner" and "outer" worlds had felt like very different—if not opposing—forces in my life. Two summers ago, I was ordained as a Lorian priest. I saw ordination as a way to reconcile these worlds.

I also have a Master's degree in conflict resolution. Although I have not been in formal practice as a mediator in some time, I still see myself as a mediator in the larger sense of seeing things from multiple perspectives and bridging differences when I can. It wasn't until after my ordination that I realized that what drew me to ordination was the same thing that drew me into conflict resolution: a desire to be of service in the world, a longing for peace and wholeness, and the need for practical skills to that end. It was also the call to maintain a higher perspective and identify a compass point to guide and inspire me as I moved through my life.

Long before I thought to be a mediator or a priest, I was an artist. I come from a long line of artists and always thought that was the path I would follow. I went to art school to become a professional artist. When my life path took a detour, I didn't see the common thread linking art, mediation and later, ordination. I just thought I was moving between different, unrelated stages of my life. But now, looking back, I see that what connects them is my fascination with what I have come to think of as the Inbetween—the place between places, a zone of high potential, of unformed possibilities, of What Could Be, but isn't yet.

It's the mix of excitement and anxiety I feel facing a sheet of good drawing paper, a freshly gessoed canvas, a wedge of soft clay. It's discovering the small bud of cooperation that can blossom and grow between parents warring over custody or coworkers snarled in office politics. It's where the friction between the material and subtle worlds can be shaped into useful warmth and illumination. It's the call to action of the neglected garden, the cluttered house, the dispirited friend. It's facing the question: Can I help in some way to make something new, meaningful or beautiful out of this? Will it work out? Will it fail? Am I up for this?

For me, Incarnational Spirituality is a guide through this luminous, promising, confusing, powerful Inbetween, where outcomes are uncertain and hope is tangible. To navigate through it one needs a guiding star, which I.S. provides.

I studied general systems theory in college as part of learning about the relationship between conflict and cooperation. One of the most useful things I learned from it, something that helped me immensely as a mediator, was that conflict and cooperation are partners in the movement towards wholeness. General systems theory describes the transitional zone between chaos and order as a place of great power and sensitivity, where the least influence can have enormous impact and result in a domino effect for good or ill. The influence that helps a system in flux settle into a new pattern is known as a "strange attractor" or seed crystal. A seed crystal is an anchor, precipitating change in a system wavering between outcomes. The quality of that little crystal can determine the quality of the outcome.

Being a priest, a mediator, or an artist is akin to being a strange attractor, someone who strives to draw out new meaning, order, and beauty that before was only latent. Incarnational Spirituality provided a kind of strange attractor for me, a number of guiding principles and concepts that have oriented me when I come face to face with doubts about the hows, whys and whats of my life and the world.

Most spiritual paths tell us our true power comes from spiritual sources. Most scientific perspectives insist that reality is physically based and consciousness results from that. We're left with a gap between spirit and matter, an either/or choice that generates endless conflict. And yet physics demonstrates that all useable power is generated from opposite energies coming together. Differentials in temperature, pressure, direction and flow are what power thunderstorms, engines, generators, turbines and heat pumps.

So I'm particularly inspired by the concept in Incarnational Spirituality of *generative capacity*, the power and potential that result from the act of incarnation itself, the coming together of the fiery, cosmic, unbounded nature of spirit and the dense, flesh-and-bones, finite nature of a physical body. We are beneficiaries as well as custodians of the creative light that comes from reconciling seeming opposites. Using that power wisely and well to benefit Earth and all who call her home is what I believe we are here to do. It is the essence of Incarnational Spirituality as I understand it, and it has become a guiding star for me.

The way I see it, we are all mediators, healers, and artists by design. We not only have the capacity, but also the responsibility, to be seed crystals and strange attractors for greater love and wholeness on Earth. Understanding and manifesting that potential is, for me, what Incarnational Spirituality is all about.

Love in Action
Freya Secrest
February 2020

Loving and being loved have always been a bit of a mystery for me. Love makes the world "go around" and is, in some way, a foundation for most connections in life, but as a foundation it requires flexible and consistent intention and attention. Love is not something to put on the back burner and say "OK, got that down, what's next?"

I have a quote above my desk from Teilhard de Chardin: "The day will come when, after harnessing space, the winds, the tides and gravitation, we shall harness for God the energies of Love. And on that day, for the second time in the history of the world, we shall have discovered Fire." (de Chardin, "The Evolution of Chastity," *Toward the Future*, Mariner Books, 2002) This quote has been an ongoing inspiration in my quest to understand more about love because it reflects something of the power and challenge that loving includes. It is powerful in that, like gravity, it is a formative principle for life on earth. It is challenging in that it demands respectful attention and like fire, can be both creative or destructive depending on how it is used.

I got lots of instruction about being loving as I was growing up. I was told kindness, thoughtfulness, and caring toward others was being loving. My first life lessons in Love had mostly to do with controlling thoughtless self-interest in order to connect with others. My mother's frequent comment to me was a quote from the Disney Bambi movie, "Thumper, if you can't say anything nice, don't say anything at all." As I grew up, those early lessons on how to be loving were refined and polished as I made friends and interacted with a wider world. Love required me to think outside myself and include others in my life and thinking.

When the first pictures of our planet from space were released in the late sixties, my sense of love and caring opened to include the planet itself. I was in that wave of social awakening reflected in an interest in the Whole Earth Catalog and back-to-the-land living. I brought my glass and tin cans to the recycling center, joined a food coop, and practiced organic gardening as early steps in my awareness of our planet as a blue marble to be treasured.

In college, I worked at my university's organic garden for a year before heading out on a study-abroad adventure. During that year of gardening work, I began to notice how the ecology of life in a garden came together, upholding and supporting itself in the midst of wild diversity. I felt a spirit of connection and integration that needed to be explained by more than just ecological patterns. My quest to understand that spirit took root in a particular moment while sitting one evening in the garden. I was quiet, just enjoying the calm after a day of work when I noticed the head gardener, Alan Chadwick, walking not far away. He stopped and stood for a time, looking over the garden. Something about his stance and gaze in that moment struck me. It felt to be a very personal moment and gave me a glimpse of his connection to the garden. I felt how the beauty, health, and vitality in a garden grew out of a gardener's commitment and hard work, but also love. That was a relationship with the world I wanted, too.

The next year while in Britain for my study, I heard about the Findhorn Foundation in Scotland with its unusual garden and spiritual focus. I eventually went to visit and found my next steps in learning about love there. Findhorn grew my experience of love as a reality in three areas—relationships, work life, and partnership with life in the world.

Firstly, my grasp of love in relationship expanded. In the shared laughter of our community interactions we created bonds that helped smooth the tensions of community life and built bridges of understanding and caring. The flow of laughter moved us into natural connections and opened new shapes for being loving. In spite of our differences of age, temperament, and background, love grew when we shared laughter, tears, problems to solve, hard work, and joyful moments. Love didn't only descend through a magical interlude or family history, it could be consciously built and fostered.

At that time, my work life was not a place I considered that love really fit in. But in Findhorn Community life, the principle, "Work is Love in Action" reflected a key standard for all activity. I needed to look again at love and its reality in my life. By trying to make a connection between my activity and a loving intention, I eventually found my way to even "love" washing windows, my least favorite task growing up.

Within the field of the community's commitment to bring love into action, my own effort to choose to approach my whole life with love grew. Love as work, work as love. That lesson continues to deepen my sense of the scope of love's activity in the world.

My Findhorn experiences also opened the door to new perspectives on a living universe built through love. The story of Findhorn's amazing garden was part of what drew me to visit initially. I was looking for that deep connectedness that I had noticed in my college gardening mentor. Findhorn's demonstration of cooperation with the inner intelligence of nature struck a deep chord in me. By reading Dorothy Maclean's messages from the Devas and working in the garden I began to develop a relationship with nature as a more conscious partner in my life.

My own connection to that intelligence did not emerge so much in words or messages but through a felt sense of joyful resonance. I remember once standing alongside of a row of lettuce in the garden. A tune and little dance movement came to mind and I moved with it. Stepping down to a next row, this one of carrots, a different tune and movement came to mind. That continued with each different vegetable and area of the garden. Each drew out a different quality in my movement, a different tune in my head to express its uniqueness. The joy I found through my appreciation of the plants themselves created a bridge of resonance between me and the life of the garden. I realized we shared a connection of love. My experience of loving the earth became more personal as I recognized and honored the life around me as unique in its essence and gifts to the world.

What I recognize now is that my knowing of love and connection opens through appreciating the specific beauty and uniqueness in all life. As I look back over my experiences, I notice that I have become more fluent in my loving. I am defining love more as a function of connectedness than a static state of being. Love is there in child's attentive play, in a kind word offered, in a community grappling with an issue, and in a garden's joyful health and vitality reflected in its green and growing vegetables. It is there in a flower's vibrant color and in a scent that wafts by on a breeze. We connect to love through word and shape, sound and color, touch and taste. When I choose to recognize and honor the many forms that love can take, I empower them and am myself empowered in my loving. Life is love in action. Love does make the world go around!

A Year of Inspired Action
Drena Griffith
March 2020

2019 was the most intense year of personal change I've experienced in over a decade. I got engaged, bought a house with my partner, and got married at the Grand Canyon. At the same time, I struggled with chronic health issues. Lastly, a complex family situation came to light, further complicating significant relationships. All of that to say, 2019 was an amazing, difficult, and painful year.

So, at the beginning of 2020, I was hoping to settle in for a time of introspection and deep reflection. Instead, a series of global crises dominated my attention. Potential war with Iran, fires raging across parts of Australia, Brexit's final reckoning, the ongoing humanitarian crisis in Venezuela ... only the smallest tip of a massive iceberg of ecological and sociopolitical upheaval. Even though I felt a strong need to focus on my physical and emotional needs, I found that I could not separate my personal sense of well-being from the suffering of so many across the world. I felt helpless and afraid.

At times like this there are spiritual and emotional strategies to keep oneself grounded and return to a cosmic center. Yet every time I found stable footing, another wave collapsed on top of me. Finally, one evening, I stumbled over an image of a koala bear wounded in one of the Australia fires. And I broke down. I cried for a billion helpless animals—koalas and kangaroos, and also the unseen and less cuddly creatures burning to death. I cried for the people dead, missing and displaced and for the volunteers desperately fighting to turn the tide. I cried for the devastated land. And I knew that my tears of pain and frustration were utterly meaningless if I didn't stop feeling helpless and start taking a stand.

Later in the week my husband and I did research and determined that the most meaningful act we could make, from the western United States, was a financial one. We donated to several wildlife organizations in Australia as part of an online auction. It was, for us, a contribution that required minor, first-world sacrifice. Yet we also didn't delude ourselves into thinking that sum was more than a tiny drop of water in response to a situation that will take countless buckets to resolve. What was important to us was that we did something. We took action, no matter how small. We pledged to keep informed about ongoing needs in Australia, and also made a commitment to get more involved in our local community.

Solidifying this pledge, on January 25, 2020, we attended Civic Saturday, a community gathering started by Citizen University and now hosted in over thirty cities across the United States. Now, over a month later, we are maintaining an open dialogue about ways to become part of positive change in our local and global communities and have affirmed our commitment to make 2020 a Year of Inspired Action.

Inspired Action, a phrase coined by my witchy colleague and mentor Kelly-Ann Maddox, is a spiritual practice that attempts to align core values with one's daily way of living and being across all aspects of one's life as a citizen of the world.

Kelly-Ann shares:

"One of the big things that stresses me out sometimes is that there's so much sh-t going on that I cannot single-handedly change. But I know that action releases tension, so if something's bothering me, whether it's the situation with the fire in Australia, the situation with homelessness in my community, the situation with suicide, whatever it is—I know that taking some sort of action to help on any level will release the tension, and it is the right thing to do. Take some sort of inspired action, however seemingly small, to align yourself with the things you want to see more of in the world. When you do that, you are living authentically, you are living in your truth." (Kelly Ann Maddox, *Housework Ramble—Coping with Sadness, Depression and Tough Times*, YouTube video, January 8, 2020)

As I consider my own continually evolving spiritual practice, I can see that I have utilized some principles of Inspired Action for many years now. For nearly a decade I have actively maintained a shamanic altar (though a college friend reminded me that I had a makeshift altar even back then.) Working within sacred space at my altar nearly always leads me to some outer act, whether to call a loved one or set some internal or external wrong right. As Peruvian shaman don Oscar Miro-Quesada teaches, "we need to grow corn and potatoes" of our inner experiences.

Within the framework of Inspired Action, I am taking these small steps further, stretching myself to sit with uncomfortable situations beyond my small life bubble. It is no small task for highly sensitive, empathic people to not only behold pain, but to actively face it. Yet this "beholding" practice asks me to not turn away, or, if I need to, to take some deep breaths and, as soon as I can, return to the outer face of the challenge. An example: periodically I check in to learn more about ongoing conditions in Australia. I look for trusted, time-sensitive resources and watch as people share their experiences. Recently my Native elder shared about the Aboriginal and Maori response to the ecological crisis and I am holding sacred space in solidarity. It's not enough to just wire money. I also want to continue giving this situation my attention, with the intention that, if and when the time comes, I will be in a better-informed place to do more.

Interestingly, this practice has allowed me to be more present in dealing with certain challenging situations within my small life bubble. There is a certain irony that, though I began this year longing for solitude, the practice of Inspired Action is teaching me that I can be deeply present within even as I actively tune in to the world around me.

It's worth noting that Inspired Action is not subtle activism, though subtle activism can lead to it. As David Spangler writes in the *Subtle Activism Card Deck Manual*, "Subtle activism is not meant to be, nor can it be, a substitute for physical action where and when such action is possible; rather, it is a complement to what we can do physically. A way of deepening and empowering our physical activism."

So far it seems that the most important components of Inspired Action are a grounded sense of self, a willingness to be present to and within world conflicts, and a spiritual or psychological practice that offers specific tools, such as shadow work, for cultivating inner awareness and consciously working with discomfort.

With all of the ecological, political, social, and humanitarian crises our world is currently facing, I think many of us can agree that the world is in need of serious change. Inspired Action is the act of rising to the moment, saying, *The world is large, complex and I am only one person. I cannot put out the raging fires across the globe. I cannot feed every hungry and displaced person. I cannot meet every need. There is so much that I cannot do. But what the universe entrusts me to see, whatever step I can see to take, no matter how small, this I must do.*

If we all embodied the wisdom of Inspired Action, our small steps might save us.

Following Questions
Claire Blatchford
June 2019

This winter, six long-time friends came to visit us at our home. No, not all at once and they did not know one another. But for about a month it was like being on a lively merry-go-round of memories, storytelling, shared thoughts and observations, and delicious potluck meals. A most welcome diversion in the middle of a cold spell.

Yet about a week after the last visitors had gone on their way, I found myself trying to pinpoint what it was that was bothering me. And what came to me was the troubling realization that there was a flatness in the eyes of one friend in particular, whom I'll call James. James has a wicked good sense of humor and always in the past I could tell—even before he said anything—when one of his wicked good darts was on the way. But there hadn't been any real darts in the two days he and his wife were with us. Halfhearted darts, sure, but nothing with the vigor and spontaneity we'd known in the past.

Then as I thought about it further, it occurred to me there was a similar flatness, though not quite as pronounced, in the eyes of another couple whom we've seen more frequently. We knew they were dealing with a difficult family issue at the time, but the flatness in their eyes called up a line of questioning in me.

What was I seeing? Exactly when did I notice this expression—or lack of expression—with these dear friends? How did I happen to arrive at the feeling that I was observing something similar in their eyes?

I want to take a detour here to say that, in my experience, questions are among the most amazing wonders in life. I don't mean just any, or many, random questions here. I mean questions that one feels driven to ask out of intense interest, longing, even out of desperation. I say "intense interest" or "longing" because I know there's a big difference between questions from my brain and questions arising in my heart.

Questions from my brain are usually *need* or *curiosity* questions. These questions are important and can often be answered in physically tangible or material ways. For example, our dog is limping badly and can barely walk. I take an up-close look at the affected leg, explore it gently with my fingers and am baffled. Should I get him to the vet right away or wait till tomorrow?

This question might eventually lead to a heart question. Suppose the dog is truly injured or ill. Suppose the limp is caused not by a pulled muscle or a sprain but something more life threatening. The questions may go further, deeper—deeper not only into what is best for our dog but also perhaps into what is right for us too. With another family dog this inquiry led to having to make the difficult decision to put her down. We held her not only physically but with gratitude and appreciation and sensed she was not only ready but wanted to go and was giving us permission to say good-bye. We actually saw her depart as we looked in her eyes. The answers to our questions were not without sadness but they took both her and us beyond pain, into release and relief.

Not to say that all heart question are big questions like this one was. Yet *action*—either outward or inward—as in motion, change, a feeling of fluidity or release, indeed **movement** is an essential part of any real heart question. When the question is answered I know it through and through. There is a rightness to it, a calm, a sense of arrival and of being re-centered.

For me, questions are quests in and of themselves. And there may, in fact, be several different quests occurring simultaneously.

To return to the concern I expressed at the start as to the "flatness" I saw in the eyes of our friends: I asked my husband if he also saw what I saw and he agreed, yes, he could see what I was talking about. This led in turn to the realization I'd seen it elsewhere too, and not just in the couple that visited us after the visit with James and his wife. I'd seen it, and was still seeing it, here then there, in the eyes of both people I knew—as in at the town library-- and in the eyes of people I didn't know, as in at the supermarket. When you begin to see something, you suddenly see it everywhere. There isn't just one dandelion poking up, there's another, and another, and another, and so on. Same with grey hairs, right?

It was as though a jumble of images, thoughts, feelings, observations and little red flags in everyday life had lined up within me, forming an understanding of something I'd sensed in my heart but had not fully grasped. With that came the memory of the instant I first noticed the flatness in James's eyes, when he was talking about Brexit. His wife told me later, privately, how upset she was by how much of every day he spent reading the newspaper online and listening to the news. Likewise, the other couple had been talking about politics—in that instance, immigration—when I saw the flatness in their eyes. I knew right then that the same flatness is in me too. A heaviness, a darkness, a kind of resignation, an inability at times to summon up optimism or any sort of hope or humor. Yup, I really missed James's wicked good darts! It was the pronounced absence of those which called up the question in me, though I didn't say it aloud: "James, where are you? I can't see the YOU that is light, lively, on the move."

Another question then unfolded from out of the various questions that had arisen in me over a few days, "Are we being drained, are we loosing vitality, even becoming sick, because of what's going on in the world today?"

I'm, pretty sure friends of ours, including James himself, would answer with a resounding Yes!" And we would agree that limiting the amount and type of news we ingest is a good idea. (My husband sometimes has to remind me of my resolution on this score.) Yet, to come to a real heart response to this question, beyond a perfectly reasonable mental reaction, I believe one needs to let the question, or questions, go yet deeper within, in the way the poet Rainer Maria Rilke described in *Letters To a Young Poet* (emphasis as given by Rilke):

"… be patient towards all that is unsolved in your heart and try to love the **questions themselves** like locked rooms and like books that are written in a very foreign tongue … The point is, to live everything. **Live** the questions now." (W. W. Norton & Company, New York, 1934)

This may sound like an unsatisfying response to an enormous question I've happened upon, a question I'm sure many others are asking, pondering, and living with too. "If we are drained and loosing vitality, if we are sick what can we do? What should we do? How and where can we find the balm, the cures, the healing?" My point here, however, is not to answer these questions but, rather, to express confidence, indeed faith, in the questioning process.

For I find that when I listen within and hear or formulate questions and make space for them in both mind and heart, personal experiences open again and again, even ripen into, understandings. Understandings on the way to go and keep going. How to live. Or, to be yet more specific, *how to **move** with life.*

The Shadow of the Moon
Julia Spangler
September 2017

We Americans have just passed through the "Great American Eclipse"—a dramatic name for a dramatic event. Like most of the country, I waited eagerly for 10:20 AM to arrive in Seattle. It was awe-inspiring. Seeing them all lined up, the three celestial bodies which make life possible on our planet was a moving moment to reflect on. Celestial events always lead me to consider where I stand in the universe on a small planet revolving around a small sun on the outskirts of a huge galaxy. Our beautiful earth is a miracle worthy of love.

As part of the whole experience, I then watched the televised videos of the event as the shadow of the moon moved across the land, welcomed by crowds and news reporters all across the country, sharing in the experience of the totality. I was shocked to see how suddenly darkness fell, how complete the darkness was, and then how swiftly light returned. At each location the event was welcomed with cheers and the joyful camaraderie of a community created simply to share a unique cosmic event at a moment in time. Very different from some more recent public gatherings of people in our country.

As I watched the news, they played a clip of Frank Reynolds, the ABC news anchor in 1979 when the last solar eclipse happened in the United States: "So that's it, the last solar eclipse to be seen on this continent in this century," he said. "As I said, not until August 21, 2017, will another eclipse be visible from North America ... that's 38 years from now," he continued. "May the shadow of the moon fall on a world at peace."

Hearing this, I found myself gripped by a grief which I still feel. *May the shadow of the moon fall on a world at peace.* It did not. People the world over pray for peace, march for peace, work and write for peace, yet our world continues to display war and violence. Suddenly I am in touch with the grief I have buried in the face of all of the news we are bombarded by daily, of those tortured parts of our planet where people and families and communities are torn asunder by violence. With Frank's words, though, I am also made aware of our collective expectation that global peace is possible. I am deeply moved by the way humans continually envision a future of peace. In the seventies we marched for peace with the hopeful, expectant youthful belief that we could make it happen. One war ended. Others began.

Unlike many of my fellow students who thought taking down the government would solve our problems, I believed that the only way to make such changes was for each individual to be at peace within him or herself, to seek a spiritual center which does not foster violence. Often violence comes from dark unintegrated parts of our past which can lead us to strike out. It is the task of each of us to find the courage to uncover those parts, to see them, name them and reclaim them as part of our wholeness. There are many teachings and approaches to help us do this, but first we must look at how we choose to act and take responsibility for it.

The shadow of the moon imposed an unusual darkness during the daylight, a darkness that unexpectedly brought things up to be examined. As we enter times of darkness when things go bump in the night, we may find ourselves confronting those things which hide inside us from the light of day. They may sneak up on us, taking us by surprise as I was, or they may erupt suddenly and forcefully. For me, this grief for my world in the grip of so much violence has always been there, but I manage to keep it under the bed so that I can function in my day. The eclipse and Frank Reynolds brought it back into the light of my consciousness.

We are in a time when the violence and hatred in the collective is erupting all over the world. Is there more violence than there has been in the past? Are we in a time in the cycles of the world where hidden distortions at the heart of humanity are brought to the surface—shadows of the collective past—so that they can be seen and dealt with? Or is it simply that with the speed of communications and connections these days we are seeing the violence and hatred more clearly and more immediately, again bringing to our awareness that which isn't normally visible? Will being made more aware of it allow us to finally address the hurt and pain in the human experience in order to bring healing to the species? In any case, we are seeing it and if we are to see a future where the next shadow of the moon can fall on a peaceful world, we must act toward that goal.

I still believe that the path to peace is a personal one. It requires us each to be attentive to those buttons which lead us to violent thoughts, words, or behaviors. And it also requires us to reach out to each other with love and caring, recognizing and accepting our differences. What a boring, colorless world it would be if we were all the same.

Along with Frank Reynolds, I also wish for the shadow of the next eclipse to fall on a world without war. And given that the next eclipse is in 2019, I suspect that it will not. But this knowledge does not have to stop me from holding the intention for global peace, and as we are aware, subtle effects can have impact. The more people holding a vision of global peace, the closer we get to it. One day, through the efforts of us all, it will be the reality we live in.

The Purpose of Light
Drena Griffith
January 2018

"People are absolutely worthless," the young man said with fierce eyes. "Total f--ng scum. Nearly everyone in this world if given the choice would willfully inflict pain upon others for their own selfish gain."

Surprised by this high school senior's opinion of humanity? He is the best friend of a student I teach, a very likable, intelligent young adult with definitive and surprising opinions about topics ranging from net neutrality to politics (he's a Libertarian) to the best way for the U.S. to handle the situation in the Middle East. He grew up on the west coast attending parties with the well-known and wealthy. And he attends a private religious high school, though he's definitely not a believer— thinks religion is a Ponzi scheme, actually. Once he shared his strong views on humanity with a teacher at his school and she, alarmed and suspicious, made him take an implicit bias test online. His responses showed no bias, he told me (hers, however, did—which brought him great validation.) His belief is pure and untainted by selective disregard. He holds all of humanity equally, on the bottom rung.

Consider this nameless eighteen-year-old walking around in our world. On the outside, he jokes and smiles. He's not dripping with evangelical guilt and shame. From an upper-middle-class family, he has seen the best and the worst that life has to offer and somehow the worst has stuck. Sadly, he is not alone in believing that humans are worthless. He could be driving the car passing us in the left lane. He could be our son or grandson. He is helping to create our future.

In some ways, his dissatisfaction amplifies a moral dilemma: at its core, Incarnational Spirituality holds that to be a human being on Earth is a sacred calling. At our core we have an ability to shape and transform experience, to birth dreams as powerful as stars. An orientation to our potential rather than to our myriad failures can, in and of itself, reveal much about our inherent sacredness. Yet it's one thing to believe in the potential of human life in a meditative stance and quite another to communicate that message to others in the world, especially when the machinery of the world diminishes people in order to sell us products and services to help us cope with our imperfection.

Concepts of self light, sovereignty, *holopoiesis* (wholeness) embody a lived experience that lies beyond the realm of the language entrusted to convey them. Yet that realm beyond is the one many Lorians truly know—and have ever known. Disenchantment and other trappings of worthlessness perhaps visited but never quite made a cave in their consciousness. It's not that they take for granted that human life has intrinsic value. Of course it does—that's the default. May it be so for all—but it clearly isn't so for many.

In my administrative role here I hear from those for whom human life seems a prison. They seek teachers in order to overcome their limitations. Or they look toward alliances in the subtle world (or gurus who can more easily move through those realms) because they believe that ascended masters and otherworldly beings have something that we humans do not. That other world, with its faeries, disembodied spirits, and other glamorized beings, holds the beauty, the mystery. At its worst, our world is a penal colony located a short walking distance from hell; at its best, it's an alternative school with a lifetime of lessons and opportunities to "evolve" so that, when we finally "graduate", we get to go somewhere else next time!

These are, of course, extreme examples. More commonly found on this path are the gently detached ones who've endured varying degrees of isolation and ostracism to be their real selves (because belief in subtle reality in general seems so far afield by mainstream standards). It took so much energy to break the mold in the first place, some don't feel they have much else to offer. Compared to skeptical relatives and polite acquaintances, subtle colleagues are much easier to work with. Even metaphysics is not immune to the disenfranchisement of humanity.

Then there are those who come to Incarnational Spirituality to affirm their belief in subtle realms, and to advocate for the unseen voices unable to directly speak to the impact our day-to-day human decisions have on all sentient beings who call this Earth home. I cannot help wondering how much easier it would be to support this desired shift in consciousness toward the subtle worlds if we also simultaneously fostered dialogue that encouraged people to reconsider the way they feel about their ordinary lives.

So how does that self-light inherently within each of us sustain itself and become bright enough to see by in the day-to-day reality of life in a harsh world? How does that inner light become bright enough to guide those walking on conflict-torn streets or wrestling with the paradoxes of life on Earth and finding themselves drifting to extremes to cope? Which leads me back to the face of the broken-hearted young man, who would no doubt object to being called broken hearted. He strongly believes that he has a firm grasp on the way life really is. Is he right?

If anyone has been paying attention, as I'm sure we all are, there are not enough words to describe how right he seems. An understatement—things are really bad! We're fighting openly on all fronts now: ecological, political, social, ideological. Reminding the world who she inherently is, reminding human beings who we really are, is not a task for subtle beings. It is a task for wounded healers, for those that life has broken completely open who will say yes to loving the world anyway. And ground that love into actions that both mirror and sustain the worlds without and within. It is a task for those who have truly connected with and embraced this most basic human truth—human life is divine life—and who can remember this and hold fast to their own inner truth while also loving their feet in the soot.

As the leader of the Native Lodge I attend recently told me, it's the people in the darkness that most need to see others' light. Those called must trust their own light enough to enter the dark. They must have focus and patience; they must remember the purpose of light. Speaking at the Toronto Youth Corps in 1972, world renowned psychiatrist and author Viktor Frankl vividly shared his philosophy on the value of humanity that still resonates for me today: "If we take man as he really is, we make him worse. But if we overestimate him … we promote him to what he really can be."

Imprisoned in Nazi death camps, losing most of his family and nearly his own life there, Viktor Frankl's later work truly embodied the spirit of remembering our highest selves in spite of, perhaps even because of, the odds against us. He endured an atrocity exposing the worst humanity was capable of at that time and walked away believing that the spark of light he called "meaning" could help us reclaim our sanity, wholeness, and basic goodness.

Perhaps the spark within the young student whose story introduces this piece will yet emerge through the circumstances influencing his perspective.

Seated in the Fiery Hope of Possibility
Freya Secrest
July 2020

My grandson is the child of an interracial marriage. His mom is African American, his dad, my stepson, is white. My grandson is well loved on both sides of his family; all of his cousins, aunts and uncles care about him deeply.

But he is very aware of the impact of one side of his heritage. Recently he came to visit and work with my husband and me on a building project. After a hot day's work, we went to swim at our local public beach. As we walked toward the water from the parking lot, he made the comment that he thought he would be the only one with an Afro hairstyle. I realized that coming into a public place for him might always present the question, "Will I be the only one with dark skin?" or "How will I fit in?"

This time he was not; there were other African Americans swimming and sunning along on the beach. He pointed out several hairstyles he liked or did not like, we swam, and then went on to find ice cream to take home for dinner. It as a small event, easily passed by, but it did open up a window for me to see the world through his perspective as he now looks to extend his home in the world outside of the safety of the family circle.

Growing up, he was an energetic kid, free to laugh, eager to be seen and participate, willing to try new things, a loving kid. Now coming into his teens, just like many other 15-year-old boys, his thoughts center more on basketball, computer games, and cars. He is still eager to learn and enthusiastic about the world.

Yet as he gets older, I realize I am afraid for him.

He has already met racism in school, as one of only a handful of black children in his town. And he told me recently of meeting the father of a new female friend. He laughed as he talked about the reluctant response he felt from the man. He recounted that he kept a polite conversation going and shrugs now as he tells me about it. That kind of hesitant reaction is already something he knows to anticipate from adults and even from fellow students.

His father tells us about trying to find ways to support him in being successful in our American social climate. "Stay out of trouble, do well in school, be polite." As a family we focus on his gifts for math and science, his aptitude for engineering. We applaud him for his success in basketball and the ways he shows care for his younger sister.

But how can those of us from the white side of his family really communicate what will help him be prepared for the other kinds of situations he might meet soon in the wider world, on the street driving home at night from a dance, or from a pizza date in town? We have not experienced the discrimination possible just based on the color of our skin. We might be able to help him fight some of the more serious racial biases and challenges that we've heard about from other families, but how can we heal any loss of trust or possibility in his future? Right now, most anything seems possible for him if he sets his mind to it. Outside our family circle of safety, many things can be blocked for him because he doesn't look like us.

The recent death of George Floyd and the flood of protest that has unfolded are eye-opening, exposing me to a wider view of the subtle and not so subtle acts of racist thinking. The ripples moving out from this stone that has been thrown into our community awareness are making an impact in me. I see how I have been lulled by the safety of our family circle and my distance from the other daily interactions of my grandson's life, from the small acts that cut away at his sense of self and inclusion. I am saddened to realize how many of those he has already experienced and am respectful of his work to navigate in his world and still maintain his sense of self.

As a society we are being forced to pay attention to the inequalities resulting from the social divides in our culture. We are recognizing that racial injustices are so ingrained in our community fabric it is easy to not see them. It is easy to minimize them as individual events and just move on. But with recent events we are seeing them in their wider pattern, not as one-time unfortunate occurrences but as a cultural norm that separates and divides. It is time to pay attention. We are being asked to notice and make choices and changes. We are being invited to recognize how much a part of our lives these divisive norms have become and to take up the work of reconciliation so we can work together with humility and honesty to change them.

I connect with these protests in a new way now, both through my grandson and through my work with Incarnational Spirituality. Because of my grandson these social issues impact me in personal ways, and I want to find more ways to meet them and contribute to healing our social commons. Because of my incarnational orientation to a sacred universe, I am called to stand in my fullest commitment to honor the diversity and wholeness of all life. I feel deeply that connecting my inner and outer actions are key to contributing to our collective forward unfoldment in both social and spiritual arenas.

I don't have any easy global-scale answers to the steps that are needed, but there is much wisdom in our collective insight that can be tapped; so one thing I can do is be willing to hold that change is possible. Staying seated in the fiery hope of possibility seems the important first step for me. Knowing my grandson inspires that kind of hope for me. Seated in that hope, I also sense the encouragement of future generations, they want us to succeed.

For me now, after seating in Fiery Hope, a next step is being open and committed to making room for what is emerging in these changing times. It means renewing my attention to holding my questions and my willingness to step outside of my own habits and assumptions to co-exist with discomfort. It means noticing my own choices and the soil they are rooted in and taking the steps needed to increase healthy growth. With this attention and intention, I will work to nurture a garden in which possibilities can grow, possibilities for my grandson and every other child on earth. Possibilities for the future of our planet as a whole.

Light a Candle for Liberty
Julia Spangler
July 2019

The other night I joined a "Lights for Liberty" gathering in the nearby town of Sammamish, protesting the inhumane treatment of immigrants being held in cages at our southern border.

I cannot help but feel grief and distress at the trauma that is being visited upon people who are seeking a safe haven for their families and an opportunity to adequately provide a home for them. The amount of trauma being experienced by the children is destructive to the mind and emotions of a young child. Trauma and brain development research has shown that children are particularly vulnerable to trauma because of their rapidly developing brain. Traumatic experiences can have a significant impact on a child's emotional development, future behavior, and mental and physical health. There is no doubt the children on our borders are being permanently damaged by their treatment at the hands of our government. I can't help feeling heartbreak about this impossible situation.

While the right to gather in protest is an invaluable tool of a democracy, I rarely join demonstrations because I don't always trust the wisdom of a crowd. As a child of the sixties, too often I have seen violence erupting from a crowd being manipulated by angry speakers and leaders. Don't get me wrong. I believe anger is an appropriate response to inhumane actions, but I don't feel it usually helps move things along, so I choose other venues for expressing my concern.

But this night I felt a need to bear witness to the situation at the borders, to be seen and counted. We are a country with massive resources, and I am among those who feel we can do better to offer compassion and care to others less fortunate! So I stood with my neighbors in a small crowd in Sammamish, Washington to add my voice.

I was ready for angry speeches. I was ready for shouting if that was called for. And that was certainly what was happening in other cities around the country—shaking fists, loud demands for better treatment of the people coming to our country for help, lots of posters. What I found in this small gathering was a lot of love. This group was feeling pain, sorrow, and love for the families trapped between a fence and a law. Everyone felt grief and responsibility and helplessness. What can we offer?

There were a few speakers defining the issues involved and the intent of the gathering. And there were volunteers who read quotes from children caught in the system, heartbreaking statements no one wants to hear but yet must pay attention to. And there was a candlelight vigil.

What surprised me was that I was participating in an act of subtle activism with a group that probably had never heard of the term before. This group connected with each other, shared resources with each other, and felt love for the victims we gathered for. The love, the caring, was tangible.

Then a local interfaith minister, Alyson Young, introduced us to a vigil process which included a forgiveness practice from the Hawaiian culture called Ho'oponopono. I found this simple prayer deceptively powerful.

I'm sorry
Please forgive me
Thank you
I love you.

In speaking this prayer, I recognized that I am not separate from this situation we gathered to protest. I am complicit simply by living in privilege while others suffer. I live in a rich country fighting to protect its privilege and wealth. I am not doing this directly nor intentionally, but I am safe while others are not—I ride on the suffering of others.

This is not about feeling guilty for my privilege. Guilt is not helpful. I am grateful for the blessings of my life. But accepting some responsibility allows me to open my heart to the dance of our world that is both beautiful and tragic and allows me to see where I can help.

I'm sorry.

I'm sorry for the fact that while my comfort is built on human ingenuity and invention which is miraculous, it is also built on the pollution of my land, air, and water. I am sorry that people live in places which cannot sustain them, that suffer war and drought and flood and despair, and need help that I am not there to offer them.

Please forgive me.

Please forgive me for my unconsciousness of those who suffer. Please forgive me for any hurt I have caused rising from indifference, selfishness, misdirected thoughts or words. Please forgive me for my faults and for the cruelty and suffering in the world caused by humanity, of which I am a part. I stand and acknowledge and own my participation, silent and intentional, and ask for forgiveness. I am human and not separate from, nor better than, any other. Please forgive any negative or destructive thoughts I have had that add to the collective field of fear and anger held within humanity.

Thank you.

Thank you for this opportunity to see and let go of anything that obstructs the clear flow of presence and intent of my soul on earth. Thank you for giving forgiveness and freeing me from constrictions that erupt from separation and self-protection, from fear and defensiveness. Thank you for sharing with me this world we love and the capacity to be in communion with spirit and with each other.

I love you.

In our unity in God and Gaia, I love you. In our shared responsibility for each other, I love you. From all the depths of my being that I am capable at this time of reaching, I love you.

As we stood on the grass in Sammamish, we could not, as a group, be there at the cages on our borders, open them up and take these children and parents into our arms, offering comfort and safety. All we could offer was an inner sense of calm, love, support and hope that may reach and help sustain them in their holding cells. Anyone who has been sustained by an inner presence during times of trauma knows this. We are not alone in our suffering, and neither are these souls on our border. We can stand with them, offering subtle fields of presence they might on some level find comforting and strengthening. God works in mysterious ways.

At the Lights for Liberty vigil, I was gifted by a group of strangers with a reminder that I am not the only one who knows this. Lorian is not the only group who knows this. Whether or not they were aware of it, sustenance and hope were offered to the field of suffering that surrounds these friends on our border and I continue to hold them all in my love, my gratitude, and asking their forgiveness for my part in their struggle for survival.

Lost and Found
Mary Reddy
January 2020

When I hike, sometimes I hear my thigh muscles thanking me, excited at the challenge of going up and up and up. I believe the loudest "thank you" comes from my quadriceps. After all, they are what I feel most in an uphill stride. I studied anatomy in art school and was fascinated by the interweaving of hamstring, quadricep, and adductor muscles around the long bone of the thigh. But the adductor muscles in particular caught my fancy. They snug in close to the bone, braiding themselves under the longer quad muscles. What I most love is the curve they create on the inner thigh and the way they pull inward, a movement back to the center.

When I hike for hours and hours, I am more a body than not. I am knitted into moments in the life of a pile of leaves, the breath of a cloud, the wetness of a puddle, the weighted tangle of tall wild grasses. I cross fields where I watch every step I take, hoping to avoid the cow patties. Or if on boggy stretches, I look for the clumps of heather or grasses to use as my stepping stones around sinkholes. I know exactly when the rain begins and walk through its drumming to when it fades to a mist, the breeze spraying droplets on my cheeks like a thousand tiny kisses.

Day passes and grows into soft dusk more majestically. Everything on earth matters. Where on earth can I sit to rest and grab a bite? Where is the safest route up a slippery, rocky trail? Now, here on earth, I am in a deep hollow walking beneath a copse of trees, sensing the resident troll who eyes me with detachment. Now, here on earth, I am on a rise overlooking the flooded river basin, muddy clay-colored waters singing their swelling notes, swirling around trees that once stood yards from the riverbank. Now, here on earth, I approach the last mile to the little village, blessedly before nightfall, walking through the cornflower blue of twilight.

Today I am indoors while the rain pounds the earth outside. I have a cold, a sore throat, and low energy. It's only a few days into the new year. I've been embodied for a long time. I know these physical ailments come and go. I am familiar with the ebb and flow of my energy. I know how it can affect my moods. The mood today is impending grief, as though some loss is just over the horizon. Is the grief partly caused by my inactivity? I have not taken hours-long hikes for many days. Is the grief related to the tyranny of habit? Illness isn't the only thing that takes me away from the moment-to-moment aliveness and love that floods me on long walks, on days spent out of doors. My habit is to feel more task-oriented, more mental, less in my body when closeted indoors and facing the return of work and routine.

Grief signals loss. The many wondrous challenges of being embodied, of accepting existence as an incarnate spirit, are intimately related to our tendency to compartmentalize experiences. Can I only feel so alive and in love if I am out walking? Or only if I have no other responsibilities tugging at my heels? No, often enough I have known moments of joy in the very routine, indoor activities of my working day. But when I have a peak experience, by the very fact of being a human in time, I later will have lost it. Yes, compartmentalization might be a factor for me. Another, that I cannot deny, is the very real grief demons flying like banshees around our globe as lives are burnt away in Australia and lives are ended and others put at risk in the Middle East. Perhaps I felt those demons knocking on my protective wall, the one I erected while trying not to sink into despair.

I spoke on the phone this morning with a dear elder family member. Age has thinned her bones and she's grown quite fragile. Three falls in the past year. Three fractures needing repair followed by physical therapy. She speaks with equanimity about her recent difficulties, commenting that everyone experiences old age differently. Her father was quick-witted and mobile until he died. One night, some months after losing his wife, he went to sleep and did not wake up. It's evident she envies his peaceful death, but her spirit is a loving one. She acknowledges the wistful, negative emotions and moves right through them to gush about how wonderful her doctors and therapists have been. She taught her nurses a song about God that she wrote years ago for her children. They were delighted and asked for the music and words to share with their own little ones. In her nineties, this woman is appreciating every moment and she is offering the gift of her light to all around her. Even pain-filled, broken-bone days can be fully inhabited.

Incarnational spirituality reminds me again and again of the door that opens to a state where every moment counts. I can embrace myself in my body, in sickness and in health. Whether indoors or out, I have the capacity to shine my human light into the world. Even a human with a bad head cold is full of grace. Even in the face of this year's known catastrophes and its dire unknowns, I can love this earth and all its creatures—love them well and devotedly. My quest for this new year will be to stand open-eyed with wonder at all earth's gifts but also with protective love and honorable resistance in the face of all the destruction. To look for the flow of moments, the very alive, here-on-earth-ness of my days and nights will of course, open me to the extremes: peak experiences and exhausting head colds. Joy and grief bookend the spectrum of fun, frustration, sorrow, mirth, comfort, pain—the you-name-it of being in a human body.

Love well that which you know you will lose. That's a pretty incarnate situation, isn't it? Knowing we are here now but will not always be. Do we secretly know that nothing is ever truly lost? In the midst of a moody indulgence, in a flirtation with grief, I hug to myself the clear awareness that I can feel this way because I know how precious everything is.

"We are never finished with grief. It is part of the fabric of living." (V. S. Naipaul, "The Strangeness of Grief," *The New Yorker*, December 30, 2019)

Could the feeling of impending loss be connected to the state of our world? Though I remain optimistic about how much we can change if everyone rallies, and how much our inner work empowers Gaia to survive this transformation, we have already seen a great loss of species and ecosystems, as well as a dangerous erosion of trust and hope among the human beings who need to step up to the challenge.

I may not be able to say what threads in my life led to my moody morning, but I know that all the richness of Incarnational Spirituality, the call to be fully embodied, the way it has inspired me to honor my commitment to shine my human light during this lifetime will help me avoid sinking into fear or despair. Loss and grief can live side-by-side with joy and hope.

Walking with the Wind
Claire Blatchford
October 2020

When John Lewis died, I realized I really didn't know him. It was a photo of him in the newspaper, shortly before he passed over, standing in the Black Lives Matter Plaza in D.C. that brought on this realization. Yes, I knew who he was and was aware in the 1960's of the Freedom Riders, the Freedom Fighters, the marches on Washington and Montgomery, then later, John in the House of Representatives. This awareness came to me by way of TV, photos, and newspaper articles. I was in the same way aware of Julian Bond, Harry Belafonte, Rev. Ralph Abernathy, and others. And of course, Martin Luther King, Jr. whom I followed much more closely. MLK's death—two days before my wedding day—was a factor in my husband's decision to do alternate service, as a conscientious objector to the Vietnam war, for a year at Tuskegee University.

John Lewis's face, in the photos I saw of Black activists over the years, wasn't always prominent—meaning center-stage—but was always present. There he was again and again like a link in a chain. With time his face changed and grew on me as he aged. And when I saw him standing there in the Black Lives Matter Plaza, physically diminished, leaning on a cane, I had two thoughts. The first was, "You may be a bit bent now, John Lewis, but as far as I know you are truly upright. You've been marching for freedom forever!" The next thought was one of resolve, "All these years I have seen you but I haven't really known you, I want to change that!" So I purchased his book, *Walking With The Wind: A Memoir of the Movement,* that day (Simon & Schuster, 1998).

This memoir is a hefty read (a bit over 500 pages.) I'll confess I lost the thread of his account once or twice because of the seeming endlessness of the struggle for racial equality. There were moments when I felt I couldn't read any more, then remembered he never concluded he couldn't take any more, so I returned to it. His book, chock-full of thoughtful observations, vivid details, insider incidents, and profound meetings with others, such MLK and Bobby Kennedy, truly changed my perspective on the year my husband and I were at Tuskegee.

My intention here isn't to write a review of John's book but to share how his life has changed how I'm living mine. First, however, there's a "little story" (John's words) he tells at the beginning of his memoir which not only explains the title of the book but truly, as he himself says, the essence of his life. John's telling of this story is well worth reading but is too long to include here. I'm taking the liberty of giving a brief synopsis.

Four-year-old John Lewis was playing one Saturday afternoon in the dirt with several other children at his aunt's house in Alabama when a fierce windstorm arose, along with thunder and lightning. John's aunt herded the children into her small house, and it began to sway. She then told the children to hold hands and to walk together toward the corner of the room that was swaying. As another side of the house began to lift, she directed the children to walk to that area—in effect, walking with the wind. Thus, the children used their collective weight to hold the house down throughout the storm. Lewis links this childhood memory to the path he followed throughout his life—a path that extends beyond any issue that separates us as human beings. He describes it as the "most precious and pure concept," the Beloved Community made popular by Martin Luther King.

What caught and held my attention when I read this book was the way John, throughout his life, walked **with** the wind, **towards** danger, rather than away from it. As is evident, not just in his memoir but in all the stories circulating now about him, he was fearless. Whatever he was facing—discrimination, ignorance, hatred, fear—he looked at them, into, and beyond them for the Good, without hesitation or flinching.

In this fragmented time in our country, I believe John's life story underlines how important it is to walk with the wind. *Walking with the wind*, for me, means trying to think and feel more deeply into the situations in which I find myself, my community, and our country. There are, admittedly—to continue to speak metaphorically—hurricanes going on out there, but I'm not referring to those. It's the local winds of despondency, discontent, and animosity I'm thinking about.

When my husband and I were at Tuskegee we didn't, I'll admit, walk with the wind. We mostly stayed in our own world because we felt as though we were from another country. It was clear to us, through the unsmiling looks and almost complete absence of hospitality, that neither the local White nor Black communities were happy we were there. Were we "agitators"? Had we come to "study" the race question, then conveniently return where we came from in the northeast? In fact, we did return to the northeast, for personal reasons, within eighteen months. Though we were young white newlyweds who meant well, we were asleep to so much that had been going on.

Over the years since then I've read many books by Black authors and, more recently, such books as *The Warmth of Other Suns* by Isabel Wikerson (Vintage books, Random House, 2010), *Just Mercy* by Brian Stevenson (Random House, 2014), *The Sun Does Shine* by Anthony Ray Hinton (St. Martin's Press, 2018) and *Between the World and Me* by Ta-Nehisi Coates (Spiegel & Grau, New York, 2015). All wonderful, all deeply moving to me and to friends I've shared them with. I recommend them highly. Yet, I feel the wind John Lewis walked with during his life, and still moves with now, asking for more. What is this more? I'm not altogether sure. More than reading? More than marching for the cause of racial justice? I believe an experience I had the morning after I finished John's book is—for myself, at least—one answer to this question.

That morning I woke to thick fog on the field beside my home. As I looked at it, I inwardly saw a figure striding out of it up to me.

Yes, John Lewis!

"Are you here—outside my house—or am I seeing you in your book?" I wondered.

John looked radiant. I was amazed and humbled he could see me and understood I was not being singled out in any way. Whatever my skin color, gender, or age, I felt him telling me I, too, am a part of the Beloved Community. I'm certain that John, even if in the postmortem realms, can see all of us and may, indeed, be looking into our faces right now with the same hope he looked into the faces of those with whom he marched and those towards whom he marched.

I didn't get an answer to my wondering, yet a thought came directly to me from him. This was the thought:

"Stay true to your simple self."

I've been holding those words close since I heard them. When I heard them, I felt my simple self: a self full of gratitude, hope, and faith in the intuitive process at the core of my being. I know when I'm receptive to those three I'm able to find my way into and along with whatever wind I'm in, no matter how wild.

A few weeks ago, when my mind was caught up in the tempest of the moment, I simply asked the wind to show me some "good trouble." That one got me into writing letters to voters who may be in difficult circumstances and may lack the courage to vote, particularly in swing states. I'm not telling them who to vote for, I'm round about reminding them, "You can be heard in this country by way of your vote. It does matter."

Then there are the days when I don't want to walk with the wind, especially not towards danger. Another story of brutality and physical assault, what can I do? I've heard my simple self say, "Okay! It's okay to take a break from the news today. Walk with the wind round the hill you live on." So I go do that—quite literally—and am certain as I walk that every clump of golden rod spinning out teeny-tiny stars, every rock my foot uses as a spring off point, every tree that my eyes greet: they are all also a part of the Beloved Community.

Chapter 5: Into the Planet

Green Shoots
Freya Secrest
May 2020

The robins have arrived in my northern garden. I walked out the door and saw five of those harbingers of spring on my lawn. For a few weeks I have been noticing the chipmunks scampering around, released from their winter hibernation, the squirrels gathering materials for their nests, and general background bird song increasing, but seeing the robins was like a neon sign proclaiming, "spring is here."

I looked at my gardens more closely. The bulbs I planted last season are now visible in the flower beds, small green tips soon to be identified. Is that a daffodil or an allium planted there? I recognize the winter aconite with its yellow flowers. A snowdrop here and there. Eagerly I peek under the mulched leaves; what else did I plant last fall?

The spring garden's appearance is so anticipated because after the quiet snow of winter, I am impatient with the back-and-forth temperatures of Michigan waking from its wintertime sleep. This energy in this time of the year builds a sense of emergent expectation in me. If I am not careful, it is like a wave that sweeps me away from the patient tending that is needed to encourage roots to wiggle deeply before exposing leaves to the sun. I loosen the leaf mulch and leave it in place. I send out my welcome and settle back to wait for the timing that the garden and animals know better than I.

So, what is there for me to do in this time? I find it is important to this moment, to sit back and reconnect myself to what I planted in the deep stillness of last year. What was I dreaming and how can I now tend to those sturdily emerging possibilities, especially now in the up and down transitions of temperature, sun and clouds, tempest and gentle breeze that characterizes the shift from winter to spring?

Most of my natural envisioning around my garden is about its blooming phase, with summer's deep greens, bright colors and expansive growth. Stepping back, I look to establish more of a connection to this formative spring garden phase, to feel into the seed and the deep richness of soil that fosters that summer radiance. I remind myself not to get too far ahead, to bring my imagination into the present moment and feel into the young, intense, bright green of new growth. I find myself admiring and honoring the small nubs of potential that are the forerunners of summer's expansion. What power is there! The seed's energy is revealed but has not yet unfurled its potential. The buds are potent with possibilities, like a wave, gently but relentlessly swelling to its crest.

Both in my garden and in my life, it is valuable to stay present and attentive to the essential nature of what I would harvest this year. How exactly it will unfold is unknown to me; like the timing of spring's growth, it is not mine to direct. But I can stay attentive to what I want to foster and, in that way, become a part of the swelling energy of life in partnership with the growth.

In my garden I would learn more about the structure of branch and leaf that frame the bright color of a flower. I want to highlight the shrubs that create the backdrop of the garden and bridge between tall tree and delicate flower. Admitting to how much I favor the blossom, I would learn more about shape and texture of the leaf and how to artfully play with relationships of structure and form.

Similarly, in my life's garden this year, I want to find more ways to feature joy by creating the space for appreciation to naturalize and spread through my relationships in the world. There are small shoots poking up, and I am committed to attentively encourage them to grow. Appreciation creates spaciousness, so even in the uncertainties of spring and the tempest of immediate social events, the diverse part of my community and life experiences can weave together in ways that serve a more coherent wholeness.

I am challenged this spring to highlight bright beauty through weaving an ordinary but elegant frame of appreciation. I am challenged to stay present to, and honor, each phase of the garden. I am invited to slow down and listen, to join in the swell of spring's life power and to partner in earth's transformation.

Backyard Friends
Julia Spangler
July 2016

Like many people, I have always enjoyed sharing my backyard with the natural critters who co-inhabit this small piece of land with me. We have the usual squirrels which raise their families in our yard, babies delighting us with their game of tag, chasing each other as they practice their skills in the trees. There is a mother raccoon who often will bring her babies to nap in the tree by our porch. I love watching the hummingbirds hover over the feeder, and the finches, nut hatches, blackeyed junkos, and chickadees on theirs. Various shy woodpeckers make an appearance every so often. But most notably there are a couple of crows who frequent our territory and for whom we leave a tidbit.

Most people I know don't like crows. They are loud and raucous and aggressive toward other birds. I am fond of crows in their sleek black beauty, though I do not love crow voices. But I have discovered firsthand how smart and neighborly they can be. One lovely spring day a few years ago I was eating my lunch outside on the porch, quietly reading, when an annoying crow shout finally penetrated my consciousness. CAW! CAW! CAW! CAW! I realized my body had been aware of it before my mind was wrenched from my book, and my shoulders were tense from resisting the sound. I turned to face the crow in the branches of the tree behind me and said, "Shut UP!" She did.

She went silent. So I told her that if she was quiet while I ate my lunch, I would share a bit with her, but only if she was quiet. Then I went back to my book. As I finished, and collected my stuff to go back inside, I realized that the crow was still there, sitting quietly waiting for me to keep my agreement. I thanked her and left a crust on the railing of the porch. The next day, as I ate my lunch on the porch, I became aware of a strange, soft, almost purring sound I had never heard before. I turned around and saw the crow sitting on the same branch nearby, and she was making this odd noise deep in her throat, very quiet and almost intimate sounding. I looked at her and said, "Hello! Thank you. I will keep some lunch for you." This contract was kept all summer. She never cawed in our yard demanding treats. She would come sit on the branch or on the railing and wait patiently. Occasionally another crow would show up with its loud CAW!CAW!CAW! and I would shush it and tell it there was no food if there was shouting. I have seen 'our' crow chasing loud crows away from our porch.

We have kept the agreement for several years now, and every morning the crow will come sit on the rail when the kitchen light goes on, her mate on the near branch of the tree, and will wait there until we come out with an offering. We enjoy their presence and honor our deal, though we are clear with them that there is only a morsel once a day. (Doesn't stop her from trying for more, but always with quiet respect for our boundaries.)

I have recently been aware of the fact that the crow couple have been nesting and feeding their babies from our largess. And I have not been looking forward to having the young crows coming into our yard with their whining voices demanding to be fed. I told myself that I would not feed them, because they needed to learn to forage for themselves. Yesterday they broke all my resolve.

I saw the dominant crow sitting on the rail and as I brought out a snack of a couple of cherries, I saw the baby sitting on a branch. The baby gave one short cry and the crow on the rail croaked sharply back. Then silence. Mama crow was teaching her baby to respect the etiquette of our yard. Oh my! I watched during the day, and the quiet rule was respected by all three crows. At one point, I saw the dominant crow on the rail, and just about four feet above her in the tree was the baby, with the other parent sitting right next to it, chest to side, stroking the baby's neck with his beak. The baby's neck was stretched up, mouth slightly open, calmed and quiet. Perhaps they were trying not to scare the humans away! Later, knowing there was no more food coming from us, they left their baby on the branch by the porch and flew off to hunt as the baby napped, head tucked under its wing. What a show of trust!

A few days later there were two more of their babies in the tree. It was much harder to keep three quiet than just one, but I could see the parents trying to teach them all the etiquette of our yard. Kids get excited when they are hungry and demanding food. I was deeply moved by the intelligence of that crow family, who have kept the agreement of no loud noise in our yard. They are no dummies. When they are quiet, they get treats. When they are noisy, they get nothing except a "No, no, no. No cawing!" from me. They have taught their children well how to survive in this suburban neighborhood by getting along with the neighbors!

I have enjoyed the company of this dominant crow. Sometimes she will come sit on the rail, about five feet away from me as I work on the porch, and together we watch the hummingbirds sip from the feeder. Friends sharing a moment of companionship. People experience nature communication in different ways, and we may never really know how our connections with nature will show up, but when we pay attention and notice our natural world companions, we may be surprised by how much they are willing to engage with us.

Re-enchanting the World:
A Lorian Priest Explores Geomancy
Susan Beal
February 2019

I learned to dowse nearly forty years ago from a dowser named Herb, whom my father hired to locate where to drill a well. Herb's dowsing rod was a modern version of the traditional forked stick—two white nylon rods duct-taped together at one end. He told the well driller exactly where to drill, how deep the water source was, and how many gallons per minute they'd find. And he was right.

In addition to finding underground water for wells, Herb also dowsed for something he called geopathic stress, places where energies in the landscape have a negative effect on human health. He was particularly interested in places where two or more underground streams intersected. As he explained it, spending a lot of time over such spots, like sleeping or working at a desk, could cause all kinds of problems—sleep disturbances, weakened immunity, arthritis, cancer, and more. Fortunately, he said, this kind of problem could be addressed in surprisingly simple ways, and he told me stories of people he'd helped.

As far as I was concerned, Herb was a magician. I was utterly enchanted, so he handed me a rod and showed me how to dowse. It turned out I had a knack for it. I was hooked, not only on dowsing, but on the very real and practical benefits of working with subtle energies in the landscape. A whole new world opened up to me, beyond what could be apprehended by the physical senses. Although I didn't realize it until years later, this encounter was my introduction to geomancy, a form of earth healing with variants in traditional cultures around the world. Geomancy takes into account that there is more to the world than we can perceive with our five senses. Just as with mind/body medicine, geomancy addresses not only the physical causes of distress or imbalance in a home or a landscape but the energetic ones, as well.

The physical environment is interlaced with and supported by a sort of energetic scaffolding of currents, grids, and vortices, like the meridians and chakras within our own bodies. These lines and grids can be distorted by psychic and noetic residues that accumulate in the landscape. Activities in the physical world leave an imprint in the subtle world. Historical events—especially traumatic or strongly emotional ones—can have a big impact and create static place memory keeping a place energetically stuck in the past, endlessly recirculating patterns that inhibit health and evolution. And, of course, there are ghosts and other non-physical beings, human and otherwise, whose presence can have all kinds of effects, for good or ill.

A few years ago I began apprenticing with a master geomancer, Patrick, a third-generation practitioner of spiritual and psychic healing. For the past twenty-five years, he has traveled the world tending to unbalanced and traumatized places. What Patrick accomplishes through his practice of geomancy is magical—crop yields increasing manyfold, dry springs and sandy creek beds suddenly flowing with water, debt-ridden businesses starting to thrive, long-standing illnesses and conflicts resolving. Using various tools, including dowsing, in collaboration with spiritual, angelic, and other non-physical partners, he works miracles that defy science and logic.

A geomancer is part wizard, part custodian, part mediator, and part Greenpeace activist, practicing in the in-between places where the material, subtle, and spiritual worlds meet and mingle with the light of consciousness. Geomancy, essentially, is about clearing, blessing and enhancing the energy in our homes and landscapes to bring about greater harmony and wholeness. Even more, it is about cultivating a conscious, loving relationship with the collective intelligence of the living Earth. To me, geomancy is applied Incarnational Spirituality.

Our relationship with place—home and community—is one of our most important and primary relationships. In these scary times, facing the horrors of climate change, mass extinctions, and endemic pollution, it's hard not to feel as if our relationship with Earth is irreparably broken. Unfortunately, a lot of environmental activism is fueled by fear and anger. Scientific predictions suggest that much of the damage is irreversible, adding a layer of hopelessness to the anxiety and shame many of us already struggle with. The irony is that such emotions are toxins in the subtle worlds, where they can create even more imbalance. Many people believe Earth would be better off without humans at all. How can we have come to a point of such estrangement from the world that gave birth to us? How do we deal with the overwhelming consequences?

That's where the real magic of geomancy comes in. We do not have to deal with this alone. No matter what knowledge and skills we may bring to the task, far greater transformation is possible when we join forces with helpers in the unseen realms. In truth, a geomancer is mostly just a general contractor, the boots on the ground for the non-physical members of the team, sizing up what might be needed, and then calling in the right healers or contractors, so to speak, especially for the heavy lifting.

Traditional and contemporary cultures around the world have held great reverence and love for the spirit of place. The Romans called Spirit of Place the Genius Loci: "loci" being the place or location and "genius" referring to the spirit that governed or tended to it. While today we think of genius as meaning intelligence or talent, originally it meant a protective spirit, the guardian angel of a person or an area. Any one of us can call upon the Genius Loci of our own places—our homes, our neighborhood, the woods and lakes and landscapes around us—and ask them for help.

While I get anxious about my abilities as a geomancer, and often am drained by the challenge of mediating between such different energies, I am awed, humbled and uplifted by this work. I am constantly learning to expand my sense of what is possible, to trust and believe more and more in the reality of this partnership and the help that is there for the asking.

This is not easy in the world we live in. In the face of hard science and front-page headlines, it's hard to trust that there is more hope for healing the world than we are led to believe. Even those of us who read blogs like this, who are members of organizations like Lorian, often have quiet doubts if not about the reality of numinous helpers, then with our worthiness to take our place alongside them and accomplish necessary miracles. It takes courage to defy the disenchantment of our world. I keep stumbling upon all the limits I've placed on what seems possible and discovering just how bereft of magic I feel.

But geomancy gives me evidence of what I long for most. It re-enchants the world. It opens my heart to wonder. It gives me healing tools that seem just this side of magic. Mostly, it gives me glimpses of the luminous presence of Love in all its emanations and incarnations, waiting under the heavy layers of despair to help us heal the Earth.

Thinking Like a Planet
Freya Secrest
October 2017

"Think like a planet." What does it mean to think like a planet? David Spangler has used this idea to introduce a way to access the stance of partnership and participation that will help us create a more *whole* future. But I can be so immersed in my own daily events that I cannot even begin to imagine the thoughts that a planet might use to organize itself. How can I develop the capacity to hold such a wide perspective?

On a recent plane flight looking out the window with a vista from 30,000 feet up, I found at least a partial answer to that question. I found myself marveling at the folds, patterns, and shapes of the land we were crossing over. I could see the movement of time and relationship as mountain evolved into foothill and from there into valleys with fields and towns.

My felt experience in nature often allows me to find the vocabulary that helps to navigate more conceptual understanding. Most often that wider, more expansive understanding comes when marveling at a detail like the pattern of bark or the color of a sunset. But the view of our world from 30,000 feet up brought me to see and feel a wider range of our evolving planet from a new and very accessible viewpoint. It brought me from an image of a planet as a neutral hunk of rock to a more intimate experience of its relationship to aliveness and joy.

Let me try to invite you into the picture as it engaged me.

First, imagine yourself gazing out the window of an airplane. The sky is cloudless and you can see clearly the mountains and foothills below. You are moving fast enough to recognize the progression in the landscape below but not so fast as to miss the relationship between its elements.

So close that they feel touchable, notice first the jutting peaks of mountains. *Rock*—just the weight of the word communicates its to-the-point honesty. The word brings a satisfying felt description of the base layer of our planet. It is solid; it will not be pushed aside. Rock can be cold and slippery and hard, but it also upholds. And with time, rock gives way to water and wind, allowing itself to be rounded and softened.

Flying on, your view softens into foothills where the flows and patterns of rock become more entwined. The word *Earth* comes to mind. It brings a different quality, varied and not so singular. Earth has learned to be collective and interactive. There are more shades of light in the ground below.

And now between the hills you see spaces of green—valleys where earth has softened into a seedbed. By honoring its relationships it has become *Soil*, nourishing, sustaining fertile ground for other lives. Soil blends and integrates to form a physical field of emerging life, an energetic field of invitation.

The scope of this awareness is wide. Rock speaks of identity and being. Earth speaks of relationship and Soil to renewal. They speak to thinking like a planet.

Now come back to an awareness of yourself. Do you notice a deeper sense of the life of our world? I am moved to be both a witness and a part of this majestic progression of life. I wonder what I can possibly contribute to the breadth of this planet-scaled experience. A response comes up in me. I have an image of seeds and a thought that says, "You add seeds, seeds of possibility that offer new harmonies to the song. New seeds to grow and shape new stories of life and your attention to the husbandry that will integrate that life into the joy of our planetary aliveness."

Thinking like a planet needs me to accept the invitation to become part of the progression of emergence on this planet, embrace the connections that shape the field of life, and welcome the changes that time and relationship bring.

Rock Talk
Mary Reddy
September 2017

During my apprenticeship to a shaman, I learned how to journey into the non-ordinary reality of the lower, middle, and upper worlds where I met with power animals, nature spirits, deities, and all manner of beings for which I had no name. My first attempts were tentative yet soon enough I was surprised by some very real alternate realities. When going to the upper world for the first time, I expected to see ethereal castles and cloud cities. I thought I'd meet austerely other-worldly teachers. Instead, I wandered as though in a fog and began to worry that I would fail to see anything. Suddenly, I found myself in the presence of an old crone of a woman with wild hair and wilder eyes. I appeared to have startled her. She turned from something she was working on, took one look at me, and yelled in consternation "Go talk to rocks!" Her hoarse voice and peremptory command shocked me back home. Journey ended. Message received.

I followed her advice. In the beginning, I would touch into a rock and get a clear sense of its intelligent but foreign-to-me nature. Eventually, my rock communions expanded to include something like rock emotion. For example, I once leaned into the cliff cradling the Baptism River as it rushed down a gorge into Lake Superior. The rock being I connected with exuded a rocky delight that I cared to visit and proceeded to convey wordlessly how much it enjoyed shedding its minerals into the river, tinging it a copper. Part of its earthly mission was to hold the swift-flowing water on its course to the deep lake. I still believe it had much more to "tell" me if I'd had the patience of a rock to listen for hours.

Another time, touching an old standing stone in Ireland that was carved with tree runes, I heard a delighted voice that said "Ah, you're back!" Then I felt as though I was atop the rock and we were flying through the night skies. I can't explain what that was about, but it moved me to happy tears.

Here on Whidbey Island, I go for walks in a Buddhist nature reserve known as the Earth Sanctuary where they have created a standing-stone circle using slabs of Columbia Gorge basalt. I walk the circle, greeting each stone. Every time I perform this ritual, I am struck by a peculiar sensation when touching the stone slabs. I feel the exact opposite of grounded and immobile stability. I feel a watery current, a rushing and waving motion moving through dark space. Some of the standing stones convey this energetic feeling more strongly than others; with one, the sensation is quite strong (the eleventh in the circle proceeding clockwise). It reminds me of the flying sensation I experienced with the stone in Ireland. I can journey to stones at a distance but the physical touching of stone is precious to me.

We humans have interacted with stones for eons, performing ceremonies in standing stone circles, carving runes on stones and painting wild animals on cave walls, using hot stones for physical healing or crystal stones for concentration of light and intention. Someone told me once that stones hold memories. Our histories and the history of the planet may be stored in stone. I wonder if it's possible for humans to co-author stories with stones? Is that what happened with the ancient standing stones? Was the meaning embedded in sacred stones through human beings collaborating with stones, angels, or Sidhe? Or were the messages generated by other beings to communicate with us? Whether collaboration took place in the past, perhaps it's time to experiment with it now.

It's been years since I learned shamanic practices. Later, discovering incarnation spirituality, I realized a key difference between the two approaches to journeying or attunement. In shamanic journeying (at least as I understood it then), I learned to leave the body behind. My consciousness departs the surrounding environment to enter a full-on trance state. Incarnational spirituality, with its joyous acknowledgement of embodiment, encourages me to involve my whole self. I retain awareness of my body and invite my environment to accompany me in fellowship. Thus, the touching of stones physically carries a powerful charge for me, as it works on a Gaian wavelength.

I love to hear people's stories of experiences with stones. And if this is new to you, I invite you to "Go talk to rocks!" (And bring your body along with you!)

Out of the Woods
Susan Beal
May 2020

My husband and I are guardians and stewards of a piece of land that has been in my family for several generations. In Vermont, where I live, owners of large properties can enroll in a state program to significantly reduce their property tax burden. For woodlands, you must have a Forest Management Plan written up every ten years by a licensed forester. The plan has to include a certain amount of logging, as one goal of the program is to support Vermont's rural economy through agriculture and forestry products.

We chose a forester recommended for his conservation approach and had a plan drawn up that we thought would minimize logging and prioritize habitat preservation in our 150 acres of woods. We met the loggers he chose for the job and were impressed by their knowledge and integrity. We walked through the woods to see what trees were marked for harvest. We let the trees know what would be happening, asked for their input, and sprayed a white X over the marks from any trees we didn't want taken or that we sensed shouldn't or didn't want to be harvested.

However, when the logging began, it was much more extensive than we'd ever imagined. For me, all kinds of difficult emotions rose up. I was grief stricken. I felt shame, as if I had failed in my responsibility to protect the woods I love. I felt angry and betrayed by the forester and doubted his integrity. I felt cynical about standards of forestry that require logging as part of a management plan—as if nature couldn't manage forests without human tinkering!

We were assured over and over again by our county forester and the forester who designed the plan that it was in keeping with our wishes and that, in fact, it was consistent with the goal of cultivating old-growth characteristics in at least twenty percent of Vermont's forests, where currently less than two percent of our woods can be considered old growth.

Several friends and neighbors railed against the logging, telling us that "trees should never be cut for human use!" or, "Logging is all about human greed," or "that logging at your place is devastating the woods for generations!" We had equal numbers of neighbors and friends complimenting the logging, wanting to get in touch with the forester and loggers for their own properties.

The county forester insisted that all was well and that, despite the seeming chaos, this was exactly what needed to happen to return the woods to a state of true balance after generations of human meddling. Over a hundred years ago, Vermont's mountains were eighty percent bare, the trees having been cleared for agriculture, timber, mining, and quarrying. Today, much of the cleared land has returned to woodlands, forming a second-growth forest. Our forester reminded me that we'd embarked on a very long-term recovery process of at least 300 years and more like 800 years. We must learn to think not just like trees, but like a forest ecosystem that measures time in centuries and millennia rather than seasons and years

Reverence and appreciation for trees keeps growing, which is heartening. We're beginning to understand their importance not only from an ecological standpoint, but from emotional and spiritual perspectives, as well. Forest bathing is an expanding wellness practice with scientific backing. Planting a tree is synonymous with ecological responsibility and concerns about climate change. Outcries are increasing over greedy, rapacious logging practices that have destroyed forest ecosystems the world over. The more confused I felt, the more the universe kept tossing tree-welfare information at me. I got emails from friends with links to books about tree consciousness or articles like, "Do Trees Scream When Stressed?", or "Join the Tree Sisters to Save the World's Trees!" A fellow in a local meditation group, a man of very few words, announced one day that there were only two things we needed to do for the world: "Plant trees, and don't cut them."

All of us use wood and paper products, so none of us are quite entitled to wash our hands of responsibility for logging. I pointed out as much to friends who questioned the logging in our woods. I blessed the loads of logs as they left the property, imagining the furniture and houses that would be built from them, and hoping that they'd retain a sense of connection to the land they came from. I checked in regularly with the woods to see if I needed to do any geomantic adjustments to help harmonize the energy

One day, while stumbling through the woods along rutted skid trails, I was feeling more and more upset by the visual chaos of tangled branches and cut stumps. Trees I had used to orient myself by were gone. I realized I couldn't possibly get an accurate read on the energetic and subtle effects of the logging until I quieted my emotions and listened to the trees, themselves. So I found a big fresh stump, still oozing sap, and sat down on it. I calmed and centered myself and, once I felt quiet, I felt the roots of the stump ground me deep into the forest floor

I reached out to the trees and woods around me and I was surprised by the utter peacefulness, so at odds with my turbulent emotions and the disruption from the logging. I felt welcomed and embraced. The trees were not upset but accepting of the logging, in fact—and this really surprised me—were partners in it. I felt their appreciation for the connections we'd made with them during the process, which had allowed them to prepare and adjust in ways of their own.

I learned many things, some of which I already knew but that were good to be reminded of: that human emotion can greatly distort or block subtle communication, that trees don't hold onto form or experience time the way humans do, and that the trees that had been cut were still present as energetic forms overlighting their very-much-alive stumps—still contributing in an altered way to the wholeness of the woods. The energetic trees seemed to have a different role than they'd had as physical trees, one that contributed in some way to the shift the woods were undergoing.

But more than that, I could feel the residue of love everywhere in the woods—streamers and pools and skeins of it left there by the love of the foresters and the loggers for their work, men with a deep love and respect for trees. I could feel that the trees respected them in return and that they were actually partners in the logging, thanks to the mindfulness with which the management plan was crafted. I could also feel the love and appreciation of the hikers and skiers who used the trails that cross our property, and I felt the forest's appreciation as well of my own and my family's love for it. The woods knew me, and welcomed me, and did not see me, or the logging, or anything as separate from its communal wholeness.

This presence of love as left by humans was very distinct, different from the energies of the physical and elemental beings who inhabited the forest. It was love transmuted by its passage through human hearts

147

and minds, a product of incarnate human experience. And I came to understand that it was very precious, a vital, potent ingredient that the trees and the spirit of the forest could use like fertilizer in creating a new wholeness out of the changes from the logging.

The trees made me understand that by being in communion with the woods while also becoming conscious, in my heart and mind, of the presence of human love lingering there, I was organizing and anchoring the love, making it more available or assimilable to the landscape and the Spirit of Place.

Beyond that, I saw that this was true everywhere else in the world, wherever traces of human love can be found (and surely it can be found everywhere!)—in the woods, in a Walmart, at a tollbooth, in an airport, an operating room, a public restroom, or in one's own bed at night. This is the practice of Incarnational Spirituality, and our privilege as incarnate human partners of Gaia.

Conditions of Sun and Shadow
Freya Secrest
March 2017

Knowing of my interest in trees and nature, a friend gave me a lovely book this Christmas, *The Hidden Life of Trees* by Peter Wohllenben (Greystone Books, 2016). In it, Wohllenben shares his experience in forestry and as a manager of an ecologically friendly woodland in Hummel, Germany. His stories illuminate the lives of trees and other observations of the interconnected "social" and ecological dynamics that help a woodland thrive. It includes many thought-provoking discoveries but one in particular struck me: that a young tree requires slow growth if it is to live to a ripe old age.

As Wohllenben explains, the slow growth is made possible by a canopy shadow of larger, older trees and is part of the process that makes trees flexible in windstorms and less liable to break. It also enables the young trees to have a heightened resistant to fungi.

I am struck by the idea that shadow and growing slowly contributes in an important way to the health of the trees. I wonder if this principle applies to humans as well. How might slowing down deepen our vitality? How does embracing all of our life's conditions — sunny and shadowed — strengthen us? What might this mean for us as individuals and how can we flow with our life systems to allow for the most resilient conditions of self in meeting our future?

Several years ago, I wrote a short essay comparing the slow food movement to a "slow spirituality." I noted then that the slow food movement advocates attention to the natural and essential qualities of food. A cook highlights those qualities by taking the time to purchase fresh, local products and then draw out the inherent nutrition and flavor through thoughtful preparation and presentation. A slow spirituality suggests that we focus on the inherent and essential qualities within ourselves and honor the natural field of life experience that molds those capacities. We can then direct our time and choices to bring our uniqueness into mindful service through our lives.

What is interesting for me to notice is that whether it is in the woodland forest, in the slow food movement or in ourselves, there is a delicately balanced interconnected system that facilitates the overall field of health. Slow or deep growth is not a single intention that limits focus, but a widening embrace that accepts and includes. All of life grows as part of an interconnected ecology that includes sun and shadow, soil and water, limits and opportunity. When we embrace the full range of our life experience with a respectful attitude, we are like the mature and shadowed forest community that prevents young trees from growing quickly. It is when we engage the whole system of interconnected life experience that we develop the most strength, vitality and sense of fulfillment. Slowing down to listen to, honor, and participate in this interconnected field—the subtle and physical web of consciousness that is the wholeness of our planet—may have actual structural implications for each of us as it does in the health of the trees that Wohllenben observed.

The shadow of a dense and diverse woodland community slows growth and creates a condition that strengthens a tree's core and contributes to its longevity and to the overall health of all trees in the forest. I find myself considering what conditions encourage me to grow "in", densify my core, and slow my one-pointed movement to build flexibility, strength, and vitality so that I too contribute to the overall health of my community.

Other Sorts of News
Claire Blatchford
October 2016

"More horrible news," says Ed as I come into the bathroom to brush my teeth. Ed listens to the radio every morning while shaving. I put my hands over both ears to tell him I'm not ready for it and he switches the radio off.

"Sounds like we're getting our first frost tonight," he adds.

"How certain is that?" I ask.

"Quite."

I think about other sorts of news as I start the coffee. Word of the first frost reminds me of the dahlias. They've been the major headline in the garden for over a month. Yellow blossoms the size of dinner plates, orange fireworks, purple pom-poms, and my favorites, the smallish sunset beauties with pink-gold-scarlet petals. And now what? The dahlias always go black overnight beneath the touch of the first frost—all of them, all at once. It happens every year and is a powerful and dramatic moment. I often can't remember, as I look at the charred remains the next morning, which was which. Was this shriveled plant tall or medium-tall? Was its flowering occasional or prolific? What color were the flowers? All individuality is wiped out in one shot.

All individuality is wiped out in one shot.

That, in turn, turns my mind in the direction of Aleppo and the bombings where lives are being wiped out daily. But then Debbie's story—which will likely never be broadcast—pulls me back into our warm kitchen. Debbie has been raising funds for the Syrian-American Medical Foundation. She told me yesterday about a meeting where a visiting nurse from Aleppo didn't mention a single name (ISIS, Assad, Russia, Iran) during her report, spoke only with calm eloquence of the need to start *every* day with hope. Yes, lives were being lost but lives are also being saved no matter how grim the news. What hope that nurse gave me!

I whistle to the dog, grab my winter jacket from the back closet, and step out to fetch the newspaper on the road. Yup, the air has a cold edge to it, a teeny-tiny sliver of ice. I zip up, pull up the collar, and slip my hands in the pockets. Pocket space has gone forgotten for five or six months now. My fingers rediscover old companions from last winter and spring: a cough drop, a pale stone, a bright penny, the cap of an acorn. Back then when everything political gobbling up the media's attention sounded like a wild, crazy soap opera and made me walk further, faster, and harder than usual. I thought that drama would end and how much wilder and crazier it is now!

Herbal cough drop, smooth stone, shiny penny, exquisite acorn cap: I squeeze them gently and put them back in my pocket. We have more waking to do together. Ha! Did I feel one of them return my squeeze? Maybe …

On my way down the drive, with the dog excitedly checking out every scent on every leaf and blade of grass, an early shaft of sun light pulls my eyes upwards to a circle of orange within one of the maples. Amazing! An orange circle within the lingering summer green of one tree shouting, "Make a joyful noise unto the Lord, all ye lands …" I stop and salute it. Inwardly, I join in the joyful noise. I thank this tree not only for its orange lollipop but for the reminder that the earth is still firm underfoot, the sky is still open overhead, the sun is up and about its business as usual.

As I turn and walk on, I realize there's more front-page news: the dog is sniffing furiously, poking and pawing up ahead at what look like a series of tiny brown pyramids emerging out of carefully groomed, longish summer grass. I'm aghast. Mole hills *already*? Isn't it awfully early for the moles to be seeking out grubs? Don't they usually begin in February or March? Aren't there other things for them to eat?

I whistle again, afraid the dog is going to launch into a feverish campaign to evict the moles. That would be the end of our summer lawn. And, hey, what's that …? A bit further on, at the edge of the garden, I see one, then two, then three mushrooms that must, despite the chill in the air, have popped up overnight because they sure weren't there yesterday. They're perfectly round and look like beautiful clean white buttons. I thought we were in the midst of a drought but mushrooms they are. And mushrooms mean moisture, so that's reassuring. And wait a minute, what's that odd mound of bumpy bead-like shapes over there beside the orange dahlias?

Ten minutes later I'm back in the kitchen with a pocketful of nasturtiums seeds (the bumpy bead-like shapes), one last enormous bouquet of dahlias (pick them all when you can), and the folded newspaper under my arm. The coffee's ready. And I'm actually already all filled up. Filled up with the local, all-around-me, find-what-you can news. The news that makes me glad and excited to be here.

Okay now—and "Good day" to the whole wide world—I'm ready to open the newspaper.

The Color of Wheat
Mary Reddy
July 2018

When I was eleven years old, my teacher gave my class a creative writing assignment. We could write about anything we liked, anything at all. I already thought of myself as a writer but when I sat down to write that essay, I felt blank. I could not think of anything to write about. Because we could choose the topic, I felt it had to be one of my very best ideas. And I froze—none of my best ideas showed up.

I put the paper and pen away to have dinner with my family. I reluctantly pulled it out again after dinner. I fidgeted, I daydreamed. Nothing seemed important or exciting enough to write about. I stayed up past my bedtime, worrying about how to start.

Then I thought about what had happened earlier that day. I'd gone with my mother in the car to pick up my brother at his after-school job. We lived on the edge of town, near the countryside. The route took us down a road that snaked through wheat fields, tall yellow-white grains swaying and bowing on either side of the road, as far as the eye could see. A visual memory of the wheat had taken root in my mind. I decided to write about it.

I had no plot or any sense of what a beginning or ending was. How could I, when all I wanted to say was how that wheat field looked, how I felt as though I was in the midst of it? I wasn't sure why anyone else should care or whether this was a great idea or not. It was just something that moved me.

As I wrote, I began to remember how the wheat field behaved like an ocean. The wind created ripples across the waving grain just as it would in water. I remembered the quality of the color—how it was not bold enough to be gold, how in the late September sun, it was a papery moonlit yellow. Words poured out of me onto the page. When I was done, I decided I did not need to know if this was a great idea or a just-okay idea. In the writing, I realized that I was describing something I loved. Writing about it filled me up with love. That was enough.

People have described moments like these as being in the flow. You know—that concept of creative endeavor where somehow you lose yourself (your ego) in the majestic progression of an inspired execution.

After all these years, I would describe it differently. (Words matter to us humans, right? Subtle differences in wording are important.)

I would bluntly say it was just about love. I had a relationship with the wheat, growing in its pale-yellow field. I was in love.

This story matters to me now because, as I practice incarnation spirituality, I keep coming back to how everything is relationship. And relationships are about love.

About the authors

Susan Beal says, "I've done many things in my life that all come down to making or finding beauty—especially unexpected—and the different ways it manifests in people, places, things, and relationships. To me, beauty is divinity made visible. I'm happiest making beautiful things with my hands and I work full time these days, much to my surprise and delight, as a bird sculptor.

I've been a bookbinder, hearing dog trainer, community organizer, professional mediator, editor/publisher of a holistic quarterly, yoga nidra teacher, and geomancer. I became a Lorian Priest in 2015 because I felt called to it. For 20 years I've been guardian and steward of my family land in Vermont and the hard, good lessons I've learned from that and from my family inform almost everything I do."

Claire Blatchford became deaf from mumps a few days after turning six but went through mainstream schools, married a hearing man, and raised a family. She has always felt herself to be a citizen of two worlds: the outer physical world and the inner subtle worlds. For a long time, the question for her has been how to get beyond either-or thinking in connection with her inner and outer experiences. In short; to listen to, look for, salute, respect and respond to both together—everywhere! Through her writing she has tried, and is still trying, to record her discoveries. Her most recent accounts, published by Lorian Press, involve her husband Ed's struggle with Parkinson's: *Rolling with The Waves: Our Parkinson's Journey* (Lorian Press, February 2019) and *Unraveling>Reweaving: Passing Through and Beyond Parkinson's* (Lorian Press, publishing soon)

Drena Griffe is a former administrator for The Lorian Association, a minister of Incarnational Spirituality, and spiritual companion. She embodies an eclectic practice drawing from deep inner wells, as well as a series of multifaceted religious and spiritual traditions. Drena can be reached at pilgrimatthecrossroads.com or drena.griffe@gmail.com.

Drena says, "Spirituality lies at the heart of all people, whether Judeo-Christian, Pagan, New Age, Agnostic, Humanist, Eclectic or Irreligious.

We may haggle over terminology, but most of us seek to offer the best of ourselves to the surrounding world. As a spiritual companion and fellow participant in life at this pivotal time, I am committed to helping myself and others shape their beliefs, practices and tools to create meaningful connections in this mundane, or even at times profane world."

Rue Hass is a Spiritual Life Path Coach and Intuitive Mentor and author. Her background includes university teaching, broad, deep training in psycho-spiritual philosophy, NLP, energy psychology, and the graduate school of motherhood. Emerging from the social/political action of the 1960s-70s in Chicago, she lived in the Findhorn spiritual community in Scotland from 1974-1981. She was ordained as a Lorian minister/priest in 2011.

Rue says, "I have a deep thirst for translating spiritual concepts into practical grounded action in the world through the felt sense of subtle perception. I love creating opportunities that invite people to be willing, heart-ful practitioners of practical incarnational magic. That is what I have learned over my own life."

Mary Reddy is a visual artist, writer, and data visualization editor. She loves to tell stories whether through words, numbers, or imagery. Mary studied shamanic healing with Myron Eshowsky, with a focus on healing trauma and guiding souls through the dying process. Incarnational Spirituality provides her a foundational world view big enough to hold all that she's learned and loved. She was ordained by Lorian in 2015.

Mary says, "All my life, I've sought to integrate the light and beauty of this world with its many dark and painful aspects. Experience has taught me that we have the power to heal both personal and collective trauma. In my art and writing, I trace routes to a state of loving embodiment and grounded engagement with all life, where such healing is possible. I long for—and want to nurture—the emergence of a new communal intelligence that allows us to peacefully embrace each other and our planet."

Freya Secrest, MSD is a Lorian faculty member, author, administrator and Lorian priest. Her background includes training in education, Waldorf school administration, organizational consulting and spiritual direction. One of the co-founders of the Lorian Association, she currently serves as Coordinator of Education. She lived at the Findhorn Foundation in Scotland 1971-73 and subsequently worked closely with Dorothy Maclean, teaching on themes of collaboration with nature in the U.S. and Canada.

Freya says, "My life path continues to lead me deeply into lessons of partnering, personally as a wife and mother, professionally, as a guide in collaborating with the inner intelligence of nature and collegially, in holding an imagination for, and practice of, relationships in a diverse Gaian world."

Julia Spangler is the President of the Board of the Lorian Association. Ordained by Lorian, she teaches online classes for Lorian as well as practical Parenting classes for local preschool parents. She lived at the Findhorn community in Scotland in the early '70's where she met her husband, David, and the others with whom she co-founded Lorian. She lives in Issaquah, WA with her husband and four nearby adult children and one precious granddaughter and two precious grand-doggers. She loves the mystery and beauty of our world, and the profound variety of people in it.

Julia says: "At the core of each incarnation is an innate sacredness that is ever present. I love bearing witness to the unfolding recognition of this sacred core in our students, the true source of their identity, enabling them to discover in themselves a new capacity to love life, love the world, and make a deeper connection to the life within it. It isn't always easy to live an earthly life, but when we know how to sing our soul's song, it can be joyous."

Glossary of terms

For readers who may be unfamiliar with Incarnational Spirituality, here are a few definitions of concepts referred to in these blogs. For more information, please see the website, Lorian.org.

The Lorian Association is a not-for-profit educational organization. Its work is to help people bring the joy, healing, and blessing of their personal spirituality into their everyday lives. This spirituality unfolds out of their unique lives and relationships to Spirit, by whatever name or in whatever form that Spirit is recognized.

Boundary: In Incarnational Spirituality, a boundary is a dynamic interface, a place of meeting, connection, and engagement where co-creativity can occur. A boundary protects but it also reveals and communicates. It is the edge of a specific act of holding, marking the limit between what is held and what is not—or at least is not held in the same way.

Grail Space: A collaborative partnership with the embodied life around us—the life within matter—to heighten and support the incarnation of Gaia, creating a vessel of energy to evoke and hold the Light that Renews emerging from the Soul of the world.

Identity: A capacity for being which manifests as "I," individuality, soul, and personality. Identity is the fundamental nature and condition of being, what distinguishes a being from anything else. It is a quality of the Generative Mystery which is imparted to the Cosmos and to everything in it, so that all creation is a manifestation of the Identity of the Sacred.

The Sacred: The Generative Mystery. God. The Unity in which all things have their being and are connected; the Holism of the Cosmos; that which holds, supports, fosters, and nourishes in all possible and appropriate ways the will-to-be within all incarnations, which are, after all, fractals and expressions of Its own will-to-be and incarnation.

Standing: To be in one's sovereignty as a clear line of attunement, alignment, and connection with the Sacred and with one's Holism or wholeness.

Sovereignty: The energy of the Will-to-Be that brought us into existence and is an individuated expression or portion of the Will-to-

Be that brought all Cosmos into existence. Sovereignty is not so much the expression of our will into the world as it is the defining and the protection of our capacity to express our will, and to be willing. And as such, it also seeks to express in a way that will protect and empower that capacity in anyone.

Subtle: Non-physical. "Subtle energies" or "subtle senses" are those that operate outside of or beyond the physical plane. They are subtle because they are not as easily discerned or used as their physical counterparts. "Subtle beings" refers to entities that are not easily discernable to our physical senses alone.

Presence: The power and expression of our Holism. When we stand in coherency and integration between our various parts, physical and non-physical, as much as we are able, our presence emerges.